Somewhere Down the Road...

Cycle Ride from Lowestoft to Ardnamurchan Point

# Further Adventures Across Britain

## on

# Back Roads and Byways.

Somewhere Down the Road By Phil Martin

With thanks to Ralph McTell for permission
to use the title of his album for this book.

Published by Greyhound Self Publishing, May 2016

Designed and typeset by Phil Martin and bound and printed by
Aspect Design 89 Newtown Road, Malvern, Worcs. WR14 IAN
Tel: 01684 561567
E-mail: books@aspect-desian.net www.asDect-desian.net

# The Plan

Having cycled from Lowestoft to Land's End the previous year (See "Downhill... ...All the Way") and thoroughly enjoyed it, I looked for a new challenge. I soon discovered that Land's End isn't, as I had always assumed, the most westerly point on the British mainland. On the west coast of Scotland is Ardnamurchan Point which is around 23 miles farther west than Land's End so, starting again from Lowestoft, I mapped out a route, declaring Ardnamurchan Lighthouse as my target.

The distance this time was something like 100 miles more but I'd had several decidedly lazy days on the way to Cornwall so it was well within my capabilities – bearing in, of course, that on that journey I had seen not a drop of rain and had the wind mainly on my back. But the Fates favour the optimist, don't they...?

Having struggled to find accommodation as I went along the previous year, I chose to book my overnight stops in advance this time. Whilst this would relieve me of that uncertainty about finding a bed for the night, it would create a different pressure by tying me to a schedule. I decided that this was the only way to go, particularly on the Scottish section where B & Bs would often be few and very far between.

Having proved itself reliable on the way to Cornwall, my method of route planning was the same – open the Philips Navigator Britain road atlas on the breakfast bar at home, work out a route following white (minor) roads and "B" roads and mark them with a fluorescent pink highlighter. Then cut out the relevant pages and place them in journey order in a map case which would be mounted on top of my handlebar bag.

The bike was unchanged except for the addition of a handlebar mirror to give me an easier view of traffic approaching from behind. This was a small surrender to the reduced neck flexibility that comes with advancing years and was to prove a real boon. On the ride to Land's End I'd spent too much time straining to look over my shoulder to see what, if anything, was coming up behind me.

Journey's end couldn't be Ardnamurchan Point because of its location, miles from anywhere and on the far edge of nowhere, so I allowed myself two extra days after reaching Ardnamurchan to ride eastwards to Fort William. From there I would catch the Fort William Sleeper train as far as Crewe to connect with a local service to Hereford and thence home.

The Sleeper was the train which British Rail had tried to discontinue until the Scottish courts refused to sanction the closure of the service in 1995. I wanted to support the campaigners who had fought for the continued existence of the sleeper service as well as rounding off my adventure in style and comfort.

*"Cycling not only makes it possible to conduct exhaustive research into local produce, it also creates an enormous appetite for information. Certain configurations of field, road, weather and smell imprint themselves on the cycling brain with inexplicable clarity and return sometimes years later to pose their nebulous questions. A bicycle unrolls a 360° panorama of the land, allowing the rider to register its gradual changes in gear ratios and muscle tension."*

*Graham Robb: The Discovery of France.*

Friday 29th August.

## Familiar Feelings.

Fifty-two weeks after setting out for Lowestoft, planning to cycle from there to Land's End, I set out for Lowestoft, planning to cycle from there to Ardnamurchan Point. The procedure was the same – train from Ledbury to Paddington, taxi to Liverpool Street (the driver of this one didn't speak a word the whole way there), train to Norwich and a final train onwards to Lowestoft. Sadly, this time the journey to Lowestoft didn't go smoothly. If the Norwich train conductor was to be believed, we were delayed by a track circuit failure south of Colchester, a temporary speed limit south of Diss and a level crossing which had lied electronically to the signalman, telling him that one barrier had failed to descend. Consequently, at Norwich I missed my five-minute slot to catch the Lowestoft train by a considerable margin.

I discovered a handy mini-supermarket on the station so I took the opportunity to buy some titbits to go in the handlebar bag for roadside snacks. An hour later, while loading my bike onto the next train for Lowestoft, I struck up a conversation with a lady cyclist who was about my age. She had endured a worse journey than mine, having travelled direct from Liverpool (not Liverpool Street!) on a hot and overcrowded two coach train. She was planning to explore East Anglia and the South-east of England.

Arriving at Lowestoft an hour and twenty minutes behind schedule I scooted rapidly down to the Euroscope, which still marked the easternmost point on the British mainland. I changed into my shorts and asked an old gentleman who looked like the late 'Professor' Jimmy Edwards to take my photograph. He told me that when he was in the army sixty-two years earlier – so when I was aged one – he had won a Voigtlander camera in a lucky draw. That meant that he was over eighty, which he certainly didn't look. He also told me that there are four ocean-going Lowestoft tugs stationed around the coast at Dover, Falmouth, Lerwick and Liverpool ready for any emergencies at sea. According to him they are on a ten year, ten million pounds-a-year contract. Whether that was £10,000,000 per boat or for all four, he didn't say.

*At the centre of the Euroscope:  "I have this feeling of déjà vu..."*

*The relevant segment of the outer ring. Those miles are as the crow flies.*

I set the trip mileage recorder on my handlebar computer to zero, climbed aboard and headed south. Unlike the previous year, I found the right route out of town straight away this year, which saved me a few minutes. Whereas that time the countryside had greeted me with the scent of new-mown grass, this year I encountered the unmistakeable smell of dung! Someone had been muck-spreading. For the first few miles I had to head south-west, following the same road I had used the previous year when I was aiming for Land's End. Leaving that route I continued westwards at first, crossing a huge, wartime airfield, one corner of which was still being used by a flying club. A sign boldly pronounced that this was Beccles Airport, though there were only two- and four-seater light aircraft to be seen.

One side of the airfield had been developed as a business park and looming large was the warehouse of Hawkin's Bazaar, the novelty gift store, sporting a fifteen feet diameter clock. This, like a similar kitchen clock I once bought from them, ran anti-clockwise (so was it therefore not a clock?) round a reverse-numbered face.

A blast from the past came popping and banging by in the shape of a 1967 Vespa motor scooter, trailing a veil of blue smoke and with eight mirrors festooned around its handlebars, which was the fashion back in those days. I couldn't see the rider inside his helmet and parka but he was almost certainly going to be a year or two younger than me and desperately trying to recapture his youth.

I zipped straight through Beccles and clearing town on the west side, I noted that I had been going for an hour and had completed 11.4 miles which, considering all the navigation stops I'd had to make, was quite pleasing. A couple of miles further on, Barsham church caught my eye and I pulled off the road to take a look. It was a lovely old building with a circular brick tower and a roof which was part thatch and part tiled.

Feeling that I'd earned a snack, I dug out a small pork pie and an apple which I bought during my long wait on Norwich station. Barsham was a delightful spot in which to sit and enjoy the sunshine whilst topping up on fuel. An old Stampe SV4 bi-plane from the 1940s passed overhead, reviving memories of a flight I'd had in a similar plane from Staverton Airport outside Gloucester, the previous autumn.

*The clock is showing the correct time of 4:02 but round the wrong way!*

*Barsham Church*

Back on the road it became apparent that traffic had increased as the rush hour got under way. It was handy following the B3122 because the road was signposted and I didn't need to stop at every other junction to check my map to see which way I was going. The downside was a lot of motorists roaring past, heading for home and eager to start their weekend.

I passed a rabbit warren on the side of the road and it must have stretched for more than a hundred yards, in soil that looked like pure builder's sand. I was wondering why they had chosen to live by the road when it dawned on me that the warren was probably several centuries old whereas the road would have evolved from a track not much more than a hundred years ago.

A few miles later I saw my first road-kill – two stoats and a rabbit, all on the same, short stretch of road. Presumably a fast car had brutally terminated one of Mother Nature's little dramas that are played out everywhere and all of the time. The rabbit's fate must have been sealed when it had the misfortune to meet two hungry stoats at once but the stoats would have expected to survive the encounter.

After passing through Bungay I turned north-east onto the A143 for a few hundred yards to cross the River Waveney, leaving Suffolk and entering Norfolk. Then I turned back onto my required heading, north-west again, through the village of Ditchingham. The cloud was increasing; time was marching on and the combination of the two was bringing poorer light. I needed to press on. There was no point in stopping to take photographs now as the light was so flat, unlike the countryside, which was hillier than I'd expected. No great heights were involved but the road was seldom completely level. Still following 'B' roads, I completed a solid hour without interruption and, on the stroke of six o'clock, passed under the railway line along which I'd travelled - 20 minutes late – about six hours earlier.

The previous year I'd noticed a definite progression in the harvest as I headed south-west but here it was all over the place. Some fields still had standing crops, some had recently cut stubble, others had been ploughed and one or two had already been spread with muck – that smell which had greeted me as I left Lowestoft.

*In six hours I had effectively dropped twenty five feet from rails to road.*

Two more miles along the way I nearly rode straight past my overnight stop, the King's Head at Ashwellthorpe, as it's actually three quarters of a mile before the village. I parked the bike, entered and introduced myself. The landlord guided me round to the back of the pub where my room opened onto the pub garden.

The room was like a small warehouse, with three beds, a piano, a dining table and chairs, a three-piece suite and all sorts of furniture. Its normal function was clearly as a family room. In view of its size, mine host suggested keeping the bike in the room with me. Given a larger door I could have kept a car in there too.

I slotted into the old routine – shower; unfold my world from the saddlebag; change into civilised clothes – and groped my way through the darkness to the bar for dinner. Although a little rough around the edges, the King's Head was still a good community pub and served up a very nice meal with a decent pint. Continuing the touring routine, I returned to my room, wrote up the journal and got an early night.

Trip mileage: 31.8       Total: 31

Saturday 30th August.

# Travelling the Dusty Road

I woke early – the usual pattern after energetic days followed by early nights – and opened the curtains to look out on the large play area behind the pub. The grass was covered in dew and was occupied by two rabbits, a squirrel and a pheasant. I could hear a green woodpecker shouting the odds somewhere nearby, too. Having enjoyed this tranquil scene for a few minutes, I gathered everything together and did the bulk of my packing so that after breakfast I would only have to change into my cycling gear to be on my way. Then it was time to walk round to the bar for a pot of tea, fried eggs and stacks of bacon which, like the previous evening's dinner, were beautifully cooked.

Out on the road, the wind was on my back from the word go and that, coupled with flatter terrain, saw me fly through Ashwellthorpe village and rattle off the first few miles beyond. The sky was a uniform grey so there was no point in getting out the camera, added to which the countryside was unexciting anyway, with flat cornfields and just an occasional wood. Wymondham, a historic old town, felt to me to be rather unkempt and, like most of the settlements I passed through that morning, seemed to need the community to wake up and look after their home turf. Perhaps the uninspiring weather didn't help it to present its best face.

At some time in the past, someone had had the inspiration and found the funding to provide large, circular, cast-iron crests at the entrance to many of the villages. So far, without exception these impressive, beautifully painted signs were dirty and had been so for so long that most of them were being enveloped in green algae.

I paused at Scoulton church, hoping to sit and rest for a moment. The church was quite attractive a wander around the churchyard revealed that there was no seat. I had a brief conversation with a passing gentleman who couldn't believe that I planned to live out of that saddlebag for two and a half weeks. His small but very insistent dog was desperate to get on with its walk and wouldn't let him linger for more of a chat.

*Wymondham.*

Leaving Watton, I stopped for another brief chat with a couple of other cyclists – a cycling couple, in fact – before turning right to start heading northwest towards King's Lynn and the Wash.

*South Pickenham Church, with my bike just visible lower left.*

After a further hour's cycling I finally found my seat at South Pickenham church, which is a delightful old building in a pleasant setting. I always wish these ancient churches could tell their story of centuries past. Most local events of note would involve the church in some way, be it hurried marriages or untimely funerals. Up a long hill from the church I passed North Pickenham Wind Farm. A sign informed me that in a reasonable wind each of the eight turbines produces 1.8 megawatts so a quick bit of mental arithmetic produced the result that the wind farm as a whole can generate 14.4 MW. A second, apparently identical octet of turbines were visible a few miles across the valley at Swaffham, so already that was 28.8 MW going into the National Grid (on a windy day).

The sun began to ease through the grey overcast and, to add to the joy, there now followed several stretches of straight road with just enough slope to allow me to freewheel for around half a mile at a time whilst watching my speed gradually increase. As lunchtime approached I paused in Swaffham's busy market place to assess the situation. A passing gent – looking though not sounding like Private James "We're a' doomed!" Fraser from Dad's Army – warned me to lock up the bike if I left it because "...there's a lot of villains round 'ere and they'll 'ave it away soon as yer backs turned". With that warning and no sign of a decent pub or café I decided to abandon Swaffham, ride my luck (and my bike) and press on in hope.

Beyond Swaffham the square miles of cornfields gave way to free-range pig farms – a welcome change. I always try to buy British pork and bacon when I can to support our pig farmers, who listened to public opinion and, most of them at least, reverted to free-range farming. The majority of Danish and Dutch pigs spend their lives crammed indoors in factory farms and never even see daylight, let alone having a good mud wallow on a sunny day.

Another long, gentle downhill swoop brought me to a small, hump-backed bridge over the River Nar which, like me, was on its way to King's Lynn. I stopped for a moment to dismount, lean on the parapet and watch the fast-flowing water sparkling under the sunlit branches of the ash trees on either bank. Had it not been given the grandiose title of River, I should have called it a babbling brook. The water was clear enough for it to be a trout stream.

*Late poppies brighten a dull morning.*

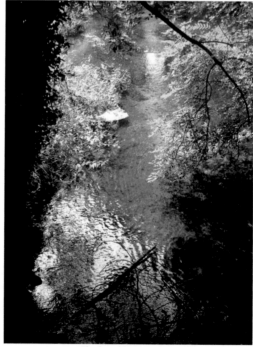

*The humble River Nar.*

At East Walton I discovered a little treasure. Outside the Old Forge was an old wheelwright's oven which had closed down in about 1940. Built circa 1850, the oven was used to heat the iron tyres of "waggons and farm tumbrils" before they were fitted onto the wooden wheels and cooled with bucketfuls of water to make them shrink onto the rims. I bet the villagers stood and watched.

*The bike, the wheelwright's oven and, in the background, the Old Forge.*

The village had preserved not just the oven but the tools which went with it plus an iron tyre and the iron disc set in the ground on which the red hot tyres were applied to the wheel rims. The oven could hold up to six tyres, three large and three small, and work was directed by the smith, who's forge was (and still is) beside the green, although it is now a private house. Appropriately, the forge – the "village smithy" – stands under a spreading [horse] chestnut tree. Henry Wadsworth Longfellow would be pleased. Apparently the oven had been completely overgrown with ivy, which had dislodged some of the brickwork in the roof. Passers-by used to regularly ask about it and since it was one of only a handful still in existence the villagers decided to restore it for the Queen's Silver Jubilee in 1977. Further restoration work had been carried out in 1990.

*The oven, with the metal disc in the ground where tyres were fitted onto rims.*

*Inside are a tyre and, on the wall, some of the original tools.*

Shortly after 2.00, having more or less given up hope of lunch, I entered Gayton and found a) another village that looked as if someone cared about it and b) the Crown Inn.

*The Crown, with the back of my bike just visible in the shadows.*

*A mostly healthy repast; certainly well-earned and welcome, anyway!*

I had the pub's rear garden to myself for my late lunch, with just a few birds for company. Ordering a second pint I started to lapse into the bad habits of the Lowestoft – Land's End ride, when on most days I sank half a gallon of ale. Two pints with lunch and two more with dinner was just nice and the cycling burned off the calories but it can't have done my brain or my liver a lot of good.

*A large, converted windmill viewed from outside the Crown at Gayton.*

Just hidden by the trees on the right in the above photograph is the delightful, three-sided, cast iron village sign. I had entered Gayton from the side road there, which brought me straight past it. Unlike the village signs mentioned earlier, this one was more elaborate, obviously appreciated by the villagers and well maintained. The photographs on the following page don't really do it justice but do at least show all three facets of the sign, only two of which are visible at the same time.

By now it was mid-afternoon but the map showed a mere six miles to go to the centre of King's Lynn, so there was no great rush to leap onto the bike. This was the plus side of having pre-booked my accommodation. I pottered around and took a few more pictures and then set off at a leisurely pace in the warm sunshine.

*Two views of the (same) three-sided village sign.*

Subsequent research revealed that the counties of Norfolk and Suffolk have a tradition of adorning their villages with ornate sign posts, which depict something of the village's past, be it fact or legend, and often reflect traditional trades or historical events. These signs can be found on the village green, or at the entrances to the village. They come in all shapes and sizes and in a myriad of different colours; they range from the simple to the elaborate; some are very old and some were re-created for the Millennium. I saw another example a mile after leaving Gayton. Again well kept, I couldn't begin to guess at its original age, although it had clearly been re-painted in the recent past. Made of cast iron, this one was more typical of the (less well maintained) ones I had been passing along the way and depicted the grave-digger with house bricks (?), bluebells and rabbits in the foreground.

Approaching the outskirts of King's Lynn it became apparent that there had been an accident on the by-pass as the Saturday shoppers were heading for home. I managed to fiddle my way through the ensuing chaos, cross the by-pass and head into town. By this time the air temperature must have been in the high 70s and I was glad not to be one of those motorists, stuck in a car with no escape.

I had planned to explore King's Lynn before finding my overnight stop but it was too hot and the traffic too hectic, so I set about finding Fairfield Lodge, Goodwin's Road. I had the address but no map of the town and so spent some time bumbling around searching and trying to follow convoluted directions. When I finally got clear directions, the last stretch took me through a shady park, under horse chestnut trees and so I arrived at Fairfield Lodge cool and relaxed. There was no-one at home but a note on the door gave me a mobile phone number to call, so that my hosts soon arrived to welcome me. Before long I was luxuriating in the customary shower followed by a cup of tea.

Having ridden only seven miles or so since that late lunch, I didn't need an evening meal or more ale and settled into the room and wrote up the day's observations in the journal.

Trip mileage: 44.9     Total: **77**

*We travel the dusty road till the light of the day is dim,*
*And sunset shows us spires away on the world's rim.*

*From The Seekers*
*By John Masefield.*

Sunday 31st August.

## Into The Fens.

Being on one corner of the Wash, I suppose it should have been no surprise to wake up to fog. By the time I'd had breakfast and changed into my cycling gear, my hosts had delivered my bike to the front door for me and the fog had thickened.

At 8.45 I switched on my flashing back light and launched into the grey murk. King's Lynn was in the middle of a large scale road development, with various roads and bridges temporarily closed and as a consequence I had go out of the town to cross the River Great Ouse via the by-pass, rather than by the intended picturesque, little old bridge in the town, which was one of those which were temporarily closed. I found my way back into town on the other side of the river, and stopped at a garage shop to top up my emergency rations. I filled the bottle with isotonic drink and put some butter shortbread in the handlebar bag. May as well boost my calorie intake while I could get away with it and after all, as emergency rations, they needed to be high in calories. That was my excuse, anyway.

As I trolleyed along with my back light still flashing and the "bottom" of the Wash about three miles off to my right, the fog was condensing on my helmet and dripping off the front. In a previous incarnation the road had been the A17 trunk road so the surface was smooth and also wide enough to let overtaking traffic give me a clear berth. Clenchwarton was noteworthy as a pretty little village whose residents obviously cared about their community – it was flourishing, with well-kept gardens glowing with colour, especially Autumn Crocuses, even on this foggy morning.

Then suddenly I was cycling past the world's largest greenhouse – or a serious contender. Hundreds of yards long and at least a hundred wide but completely empty, it was either between crops or brand new. I reckoned the latter as it was in absolutely pristine condition. If size was anything to go by they certainly planned to grow a lot of something.

A couple of miles up the road I had to rejoin the A17 in order to cross the River Nene at Sutton Bridge. No sooner had I crossed onto the main road than I entered Lincolnshire, where I was greeted with rather a mixed message...

*"You can come in but behave yourself!"   At least the fog was thinning.*

A mile of main road brought me to Sutton Bridge, where there were many interesting things to see; firstly, the bridge itself – more properly called Cross Keys Bridge. It was built in 1897 as a railway swing bridge but now carries the traffic on the A17, which it cleverly removes from the path of ships and yachts heading along the River Nene to and from the inland port of Wisbech.

Unmistakeably Victorian, it shouts its strength at you with thousands of hand hammered rivets and no concession to elegance or daintiness. I don't suppose that many ladies would find it beautiful but I know many men, me included, who would happily spend an hour or two exploring its workings and construction. We must have been half way through an ebb tide because the water was racing under the bridge towards the Wash at a rate of knots, in dramatic contrast to the still, grey morning.

Beside the bridge is a memorial consisting of a single, bent aircraft propeller blade mounted on a plinth. A plaque announces:

*"This memorial is dedicated to all members of the Royal Air Force of all nationalities who served at RAF Sutton Bridge from*
*1926 to 1958".*

I wonder if the propeller blade was already bent when erected or if it was the result of mindless vandalism. It did look like the result of a wheels-up landing or an aircraft tipping onto its nose.

Leaving the bridge behind, I passed through the actual village of Sutton Bridge – formerly a seaport – and headed into Hereward the Wake country. I tried to visualise it as it was in his day – pre drainage and agriculture – endless miles of flat, misty fenland. I don't envy those Norman soldiers (and the Romans before them) trying to stamp their authority on these godless, featureless marshes. Apparently the Fens were rich in marine life, particularly eels, which were so highly prized that they were not only caught for food but were used as local currency in earlier times. In addition, the fens have always supported a vast variety of birdlife. Dwellers in the fens harvested reeds, peat, and rushes for sale, and so essential were these natural materials to the economy of the area in medieval times that their harvest was carefully controlled by powerful, local landowners.

*I could imagine the two railway lines with a train in place of the car.*
*Note the bridge operator on his balcony, through the left hand arch.*

*Possibly a better picture without the large telegraph pole and the paving slab.*

The Romans planned to drain the fens but got no further than building a dyke to keep the sea at bay. Queen Elizabeth 1st had similar ambitions which came to nought and it wasn't until the 17th Century that the Duke of Bedford made a real start. He attracted investors to the scheme and called in the experienced Dutch engineer Cornelius Varmuyden, who started work in 1626.

Varmuyden's work received a setback during the Civil War when, in 1642, Cromwell's forces broke his dykes in an attempt to re-flood the land in order to thwart a Royalist advance. (The Roundheads seem to have been very enthusiastic about massive destruction and desecration, using war as their excuse). At the end of the Civil War, following the execution of King Charles 1 in 1649, work restarted with labour provided by Scottish and Dutch prisoners of war.

Crossing Fenland is rather like travelling over that other great area of drained marshland, the Somerset Levels – every few hundred yards one crosses a drainage channel or stream. Most of them, being man-made, are as straight as a die and they are used in lieu of hedges or fences to delineate fields and meadows, giving a very open, unrestricted view across the landscape. It occurred to me that in Hereward's day this would have been a really desolate wilderness and very intimidating to outsiders. In the damp mist I reckoned that this "improved" version was depressing enough.

It was a few miles from here in 1216, that King John lost his treasure in the Wash, several miles inland from the present day shoreline. That realignment, no doubt, is due to 800 years of the aforementioned improvements in land drainage forcing back the sea. Historians still argue over the veracity of the story but if it's true, he lost not only the entire royal treasury but his regalia, his wardrobe and two to three thousand soldiers and servants. Careless! Apparently they took a short cut across the Nene estuary (some say it was the Welland estuary, farther north) to save nine miles while the king and his immediate entourage, moving more swiftly, went the long (and safe) way round through Wisbech. If you know your history, 1216 was the second bad year in a row for King John as the previous year he'd been coerced into signing the Magna Carta at Runnymede. To top it all, a few months after losing his treasure, he died at Newark.

*The town sign at the entrance to Long Sutton.*

After passing through Long Sutton and crossing the A17 (again) I stopped to shed my long-sleeved jersey beside a rose nursery, across which ran a power line whose wires supported several hundred chattering starlings. The lines of roses brought a welcome splash of colour to this drab morning.

Just down the road I discovered the remains of Gedney railway station, complete with parts of the original platforms and still defiantly sporting the large, overgrown wooden platform sign (not visible in the photograph). It was closed in 1959, along with the former Midland & Northern Joint Railway of which it was part.

Leaving Gedney station, it dawned on me that I was heading south, rather than the northwest which my route demanded. Oops! The map showed an easy short cut to get back on track and I reckoned the small joys on which I'd stumbled justified the extra mile of pedalling. I paralleled the A17 for a couple of miles through Gedney village and Fleet Hargate and then crossed it yet again before taking a refuelling break at Cackle Hill. I munched some shortbread at the roadside whilst watching the traffic on the main road, not far away across the fields. Half a mile up the road I crossed the Greenwich Meridian. No marker post this time or, if there was, I failed to spot it. Unlike my ongoing relationship with the A17, this was a once and only crossing shortly before I entered the village of Saracen's Head. At the entrance to that village was an apt, imposing, stone carving of Saladin created by Richard Holliday and unveiled in 1999.

*A family gathering outside the village hall in Saracen's Head.*

*St Peter & St Paul, Algarkirk, in its rather unkempt churchyard.*

In Saracen's Head was the village pub of the same name, which caused me to wonder about the chicken-and-egg situation which this revealed. An Internet search was fruitless: apparently no-one knows which name came first, pub or village name.

I continued my flirtation with the A17, crossing, re-crossing and once joining it to cross the River Welland on the Fosdyke Bridge. This was not just Hereward the Wake country, this was Viking country – many village names were clearly of Scandinavian origin, for example Algarkirk, Wigtoft, Skeldyke and Sandholme.

*The remains of Wigtoft Windmill: once upon a time a major landmark.*

*Off the beaten track: a typical fenland lane.*

Then I had a real scare – I went to take a photograph and was greeted by a blank viewfinder. (My camera is a digital SLR, which means that the viewfinder sees the actual electronic image which the camera will record). I switched it off and on again but no joy. Removing and replacing the memory card made no difference, either.

Hell! No more photos for at least twenty two hours – this being Sunday morning – until I could find a repairer or a replacement and that would mean diverting into a decent sized town. Nothing for it but to crack on. Then, a couple of miles along the road I had a brainwave. Those of a less kindly persuasion would say I actually started to think clearly. I stopped and got out the camera. Hey Presto – my hunch was right – the function selector switch was stuck midway between two settings and thus sending the images precisely nowhere! A quick flick and I was back in business. Not a disaster but one missed photo.

Having drunk four cups of tea at the B&B I had skipped coffee and was now ready for lunch. I thought I'd found it at the Golden Fleece in Wigtoft but they didn't serve food so I pressed on. I felt a drop of rain on my thigh and, sure enough, it began spotting from the flat, grey sky. Nothing to worry about for the moment but was it a portent?

Reaching Swineshead I paused outside a tempting hotel which offered food and ale but, with not that far to go, decided to phone ahead to my next night stop and see if they provided evening meals. Switching on the phone brought in a flood of stored texts and calls from Sue which occupied me for a while and then I made the call and found that the B&B did indeed serve cooked meals.

Having realised that on the Land's End trip I had consumed half a gallon of ale on most days, I decided to skip the pub lunch and went into the shop next door. (This would also save time in case the rain came on again). Buying a Cornish pasty, a Belgian apple cake and a drink, I went across the road to sit in Swineshead churchyard and dine al fresco. Finding no seat in the churchyard I enjoyed my lunch perched on the hard, stone, second step of the belfry's exterior staircase instead.

Preparing to resume my journey, I discovered that the next page of my map system was missing. A few minutes' investigation confirmed that it *was* actually missing and not simply out of place. I was lost in the wilds of Lincolnshire! I quickly deduced that the current page showed me about to either join or cross the good old A17 and the next page showed me leaving it – for the last time, incidentally – and heading north.

The easy way out of my predicament was to seize this last chance to actually join the A17. This meant that I was able to thrash along at nearly 20 mph for several miles until I spotted the turn-off for South Kyme (my destination) as the main road veered round to the west. Once out on the peaceful fens I paused to look around. Visibility was about three miles with just the barest breath of wind and it was still trying to rain. The water level in the dykes was eight feet below field level – so definitely drainage and not irrigation - and ten feet below the slightly elevated road.

Having told the pub that I would arrive mid to late afternoon, I found myself in South Kyme a little after 2.00 o'clock. I explored the elaborate, wrought iron monument to the bi-centenary of the Slea Navigation. It sits beside Kyme Eau, which becomes the River Slea and flows into the Wash through Boston, off to the east.

I ventured down a little side lane but when it brought me out directly opposite the Hume Arms, my chosen stop for the night, I took this as an omen and went in. My room wasn't ready but, God bless them, they welcomed me in and had the room ready in ten minutes. And so I could escape the days near 100% humidity and immerse myself in a shower. After the usual rigmarole of unpacking and having my customary cup of tea I went out to explore South Kyme on foot.

*The Hume Arms, the bridge over Kyme Eau and (from the pub) the Old Smithy.*

*The last of four towers which formed the corners of the 14ᵗʰ Century castle. The stone from the rest of the castle is to be found in many local buildings so maybe recycling is not such a modern concept after all!*

*The Norman church of St Mary and All Saints (or All Angels) at South Kyme was considerably re-built in 1805 and restored in 1890.*

I found my way up the bank of Kyme Eau and was startled to discover a castle tower appearing through a gap in the trees on the far bank. It is the last remnant of what was once an impressive castle, built in the 14th Century on a Saxon site. A frightened cow is reputed to have run all the way up the stairs of the castle, though not the spiral staircase of one of the 77ft towers, I'm quite sure!

A convenient bridge allowed me to cross Kyme Eau and walk back past the tower to the parish church, the sturdy construction of which shows its Norman origins. The 19th Century windows sit surprisingly well in its walls and their installation must have made a huge difference to light levels inside the church.

After an hour or so the rain began in earnest so I made my way back to the welcome shelter of the Hume Arms. After swapping texts with Sue I wrote up my journal and went down to the bar for a dinner of "Italian Beef". This comprised strips of fillet steak in a tomato, onion and mushroom sauce on a bed of rice and was delicious.

Trip mileage   46.1        Total   123

*My bed, scattered with assorted personal clutter.*

Monday 1st September.

## A Slight Change of Plan

I awoke to clear skies and sunshine and the view from the window was transformed from the previous day. Landlord Kieran, the only person there apart from myself cooked my breakfast and did me proud. I wanted to put some miles behind me while the weather was good and so I was on the road by 9.00 o'clock. I left £10 for the staff kitty as a thank you for the warm welcome and rapid preparation of my room after my premature arrival. Once I cleared South Kyme's trees the countryside was so flat and the air so clear that the view was limited only by the Earth's curvature. A south-westerly breeze pushed me along the road with several stops for photography in the clear sunshine.

Five miles up the road I noticed the first, gentle undulations in the terrain (and the road). The thought occurred to me that I would miss the flat fens when I was attacking the northern hills. Another ten miles and the undulations were becoming more pronounced. It seemed I was leaving the fens behind already. Somewhere ahead and to my left was an airfield where Hercules aircraft were flying circuits. I pondered the progression of a developing pilot from 2-seater trainer to huge, four-engined transport aircraft. I'm sure that a flight simulator features in the process at some stage.

Having recently seen two dead stoats on the road, it was nice to have a live one run across in front of me and make a high leap into the long grass on the verge. A little further along I saw a second one, which balanced the books rather nicely.

Approaching Metheringham I was surprised to see a strange, four tracked tractor pulling a plough which incorporated *ten* shares (blades). It sounded as powerful as it obviously was – if you have a large, flat field; don't mess about with half measures. Impressed, I rattled off a couple of pictures. Back on the bike, I rode over a level crossing on the Sleaford to Lincoln railway line. It was an old fashioned, manually operated one with a traditional crossing keeper's box – a nice little piece of nostalgia.

*The sunlit view from my room window which heralded the dawn.*

*Looking back at South Kyme's Norman church in the morning sunshine.*

*The distant horizon.   A dramatic contrast to the mist of the day before.*

*A powerful piece of kit – one pass would turn over our whole garden at home.
This photograph was to bring me an inordinate amount of grief.*

*The signpost which caught my eye, leading to an important discovery.*

Once in Metheringham, I made the spur of the moment decision to make a small detour through the little village of Dunston, just a mile up the road. This took me back over the railway, via a bridge this time. The village justified the deviation from route – it was very pretty, with some beautiful gardens of late summer flowers. The road out to rejoin the official route took me back over the railway for a third time and then two more right turns brought rail crossing number four. Shades of my old friend, the A17.

This last right turn set my back to the south-west wind so that I could finally feel its full benefit. I could now look forward to seven or eight miles of wind assistance. The effect was immediate – with a slight down slope I found myself freewheeling at 22 mph into Nocton. Beyond the village I noticed a signpost for the hamlet of Wasps Nest. That certainly merited a photo so I coasted to a halt at the best vantage point.

I lifted the camera out of the handlebar bag and took the picture. Replacing the camera it dawned on me that my wallet wasn't in its usual place at the top of the bag. Where had I put it this time? There weren't many places where it could be. I checked the pockets on my cycling vest and on the jumper which I'd shed earlier. No joy. It hadn't worked its way further down into the handlebar bag. I knew it wasn't in either of the saddlebag side pockets but checked anyway. No joy.

I had lost my wallet. I had also, therefore, lost £80 in cash, my credit and debit cards, all of the various other cards which lived in there and my ticket for the Fort William Sleeper train which had cost me £135 on its own. All of this was of course impossible, so I double checked. It turned out that not only was it possible but it had happened. My brain raced around the ramifications of my situation, which was clearly very serious, as well as being a result of my own undoubted carelessness.

I could go no further. I had my cheque book in the saddlebag but it was useless without the bank guarantee card which was in the lost wallet. First move was to phone back to the Hume Arms and ask Kieran if I'd left it there after settling my account. His quick check knocked that one on the head and so I asked him if the room was still free if needed – it was.

Pretty obviously the wallet had been flicked out of the handlebar bag by the trailing camera strap at one of my photo-stops. I turned round and headed back towards South Kyme to check all of the places where I had taken pictures. I had covered 16.5 miles, so there was time to get back on track and make up lost time if I found the wallet fairly quickly. I set a good pace and rocketed back through Metheringham, churning over the possibilities. There was a most likely prospect – at one stop, about half way back to the pub, the bike had tried to fall over and I had only just saved it from doing so – but I arrived there to find nothing. I checked each photo-stop as I came to it, bearing in mind that several were just random pauses at the side of the road.

It doesn't affect the story to tell you now that in my haste I shot straight past just one stop and that was the one where my wallet was lying on the grass. (For the curious, it was found two months later where I photographed the tractor with the ten bladed plough, only five miles back along my route). The wisdom of hindsight suggests that, having established the likely cause of my loss, the logical thing to do would have been to review the photos on the camera and visit the site of each one in turn as I retraced my morning's ride. But as the saying goes, hindsight is a wonderful thing!

At Billinghay I spotted a police car and waved it down. The two bobbies inside were very reluctant to get involved and just gave me a card containing the phone number of their headquarters at Lincoln. Back at the Hume Arms, after a very sympathetic welcome, I started the process of stopping bank and credit cards and trying to formulate a plan. I also needed to enlist Sue's help back in Herefordshire. There was no mobile signal at the pub and I was advised to stand on the river bridge across the road from the front door, where there was a usable signal.

The credit card company answering robot had me answering multiple choices and then waiting in a queue for twelve minutes – a long time when you're stressed – before I got through to a real person and stopped the card. They automatically arranged a replacement card but when I arrived home I closed the account *and* told them why. My bank, First Direct, answered promptly and were brilliant and I was able to arrange to collect a huge sum of cash from the nearest HSBC branch, at Sleaford, the next morning.

At the same time Sue was phoning First Scotrail to arrange for a replacement train ticket to be sent ahead of me for collection at the end of my journey. She spent some time beating her head against the brick wall of a company who will replace a stolen ticket but not a lost one. Silly though this policy is, they wouldn't budge.

Gradually I saw the emergence of a chance to carry on and save the sponsorship money as well as my self esteem. The sponsors were important because several of them had trustingly invested their money in the ride ahead of my departure. I rang my next planned night stop and cancelled the booking.

To retrieve the situation I would have to travel by train from the nearest station, at Sleaford, to within striking distance of the following night's stay at Pocklington. It remained to be seen whether the railway system could rise to the challenge and also whether I could bluff my way onto the Fort William Sleeper in a week and a half's time.

It had been a long, exhausting day.


Trip mileage: 32.9        Total:  156


Day's progress towards Ardnamurchan Point:        0!


*A man without a challenge or ambition is still a boy.*

*Barry Smith*

# Tuesday 2nd September.

## Let the Train Take the Strain.

I breakfasted with crossed fingers, since the whole of the rest of the journey depended on the outcome of today's events. I had a good start when Kieran waived my room fee and only charged me a nominal £20 for my food and drink, bearing in mind that this was for lunch, dinner *and* breakfast. It was a relief to climb back on the bike at last and ride off into the sunshine towards Sleaford, eight miles to the west. I had woken to heavy cloud, with blue sky about ten miles distant and, exactly as forecast; the back edge of the cloud and therefore the front edge of the blue sky, had crept towards South Kyme to arrive shortly before my departure.

It had been a long Monday afternoon; firstly with the frustrations of dealing with the banks via a dodgy phone signal, then formulating a plan and finally sitting in an empty room trying to think of anything I'd missed and wondering if everything really was going to fall back into place. It had cost almost £20 on my mobile phone, choosing Option 2, then Option 4, then another Option 2 and then listening to a robot telling me, every minute and a half, how important my call was to the credit card company.

Now the portents were good. Behind me were heavy grey clouds while ahead of me was clear blue sky and sunshine. I could almost hear the Walt Disney heavenly choir. As I settled into the rhythm of the bike I began to take an interest in my surroundings for the first time in twenty two hours. Beside the road was a newly ploughed field and the soil was a rich, dark brown; as dark as a chocolate fudge cake (on which I'm something of an expert) and looking very fertile.

Arriving in Sleaford, a pleasant town with a complex one-way system (which does actually work quite well) I took a while to find the HSBC branch. Eventually I asked for directions (and we know how difficult *that* is for us men) from a passer-by who looked perplexed and said he'd no idea. And then I spotted the bank almost directly opposite where we were standing.

*The approach to Sleaford town centre.*

For security purposes I was under instructions to phone First Direct from outside the bank. When I did so I spoke to Gillian, who was an absolute star. Having sorted the security aspects, she asked all about the bike ride and why I was doing it, sounding genuinely interested. When I'd given her a potted version of the plan and the story so far she wished me luck, sounding as if she really meant it and boosting my morale enormously.

I joined the queue inside and when it came to my turn, the information on the branch's computers was out of date. They (we!) had to make two more calls to First Direct to rectify the situation. However I eventually left the bank with an envelope stuffed with £20 notes and hurried into town to buy a wallet and a road atlas. The road atlas was necessary because the nearest mainline railway station to my next overnight stop, Pocklington, was Selby and I had no map of the road system between the two. I simply couldn't afford to bumble about and hope to find my way there. Strangely, a road atlas was cheaper than a detailed local map.

So – don't tell Friends of The Earth – I bought a wallet and the cheapest atlas I could find, tore out the one page that I needed and dumped the rest in a waste bin. Needs must when the Devil drives and there was no way I could cart something of that bulk and weight along with me for the rest of the journey.

Having bought these essential items, I went to the station to see how the land lay. My son Andy had done some research online and texted me with useful information on train routes and alternative destinations, including Selby being my best bet, but I would still be relieved to see the details on a station timetable.

As I entered the station a train was standing at the platform. The conductor was standing by it so I seized the opportunity to pick his brains about my predicament. He poked away at his ticket machine for a few minutes and then, miraculously it seemed to me, he printed out a "ticket" for me with full details of the quickest journey to Selby. It wasn't via Grantham, as the internet had suggested, but via changes of train at Lincoln and Retford.

The first thing was to buy a ticket, which my conductor friend was unable to supply – odd when his ticket machine had provided the journey details. I went to the station ticket office and stood behind a couple who were being served. The ticket clerk immediately informed me over their shoulders that she wasn't serving anyone else for the next twenty minutes. Ah yes, customer service – I remember that. A hand-written note on the glass confirmed that the ticket office was closed from 11.00 to 11.20 and so I nipped back into town to buy snacks and a drink for my lunch.

Returning to the station I found seven people queuing at the (still closed) ticket window. 11.20 came and went and the blind remained down. At 11.23, ten minutes before my train was due to leave and with eight customers to serve, the blind went up and the truculent looking ticket clerk gazed blankly at her first customer. He didn't want a ticket; he wanted information. His sister was travelling up from Shoreham and he wanted details for her journey. He was still standing there with five minutes to go to my train's departure time so I gave up and carried my bike over the footbridge to Platform 3.

The train arrived a couple of minutes late and I heaved the bike into one end of the single, solitary carriage. The cycle storage area was full of suitcases so I stood and held the bike upright. In this one paragraph you have the best and the worst of the railway experience in this country: the efficient, interested and friendly conductor, the surly ticket clerk whose coffee break was the only thing that mattered to her and a single carriage train with standing room only.

It seems that train conductors are a breed apart – I now met the second of three stars of that profession whom I was destined to meet that day. This one, a friendly lady, sold me a ticket to Selby for £35. It was then that I realised that, with my wallet, I had also lost my railcard which would have saved me more than ten pounds on that transaction alone.

As we rattled northward, re-crossing yesterday's level crossing and three bridges – under them this time – for the third time, I passed within six hundred yards of the lost wallet, which was still lying where it had fallen. I noticed a Boeing AWACS aircraft flying over with its huge, revolving radar scanner on top. If I'd been on the bike I would undoubtedly have taken a photo. Had I been on the bike, however, I wouldn't have been there. I would have been crossing the Humber Bridge which I would now miss: another consequence of my carelessness. Entering Lincoln station I caught my first ever glimpse of Lincoln Cathedral. Sadly it was very brief and through a dirty train window, so the resulting hurried attempt at a photo produced a rather dire result. My second train of the day was also just a single carriage but it was waiting, almost empty at the platform so I secured the bike and made the most of the chance to sit down.

The journey to Retford was mainly noteworthy for the end of Fenland and the first real hills that I'd seen since starting my journey. Alighting onto one of only two platforms at Retford, I asked the conductor if the Selby train would come in on the same platform. "No" he said, "There are two stations. Up the steps" and grinned at me. I picked up the bike. Sure enough the (many) steps led to a much bigger, much higher station with multiple tracks between the two long platforms. An HST blasted through at 125 mph and frightened me half to death – I had been carefully avoiding the 21$^{st}$ Century pace of life for the past four days.

Finding the ticket office I asked if the bike would need a ticket for this final leg of the journey. "Yes" came the dour reply "But I can't sell you one. You need to apply to Hull Trains". Never mind all that – I took the bike to the far platform via a welcome pair of lifts and a subway. When the train came in there was no sign of a conductor so I quickly lifted the bike in through the special, wide, cycle door. The cycle compartment was locked so I parked the bike in the door well and sat where I could keep an eye on it.

When the young conductress came along checking tickets, I asked about a ticket for the bike. "Don't bother" she said "It'll be fine. Do you want to put it in the compartment?" I declined, since that would mean removing saddlebag and handlebar bag, only to re-attach them later. A while later I heard her announce the stops for the rest of the journey and only then did I realise that the train would turn east at Selby and head for Hull. It would call at Brough, only two and a half miles from the pink line on my map!

I sought out the conductress and asked for an extension ticket for Brough. "Don't bother – it would only be a few pence – just stay on the train". This led to an explanation of why I wanted to go to Brough and, like everyone, she wished me well for the rest of my journey. When I emerged from the back of the train at Brough she gave me a big, morale-boosting wave goodbye from the front of the train, along the whole length of the platform. She was star number three in the train conductor firmament. It still brings a lump to my throat to remember that wave.

At last I was back under my own steam and roughly where I should be. I went to take a first and last look at the River Humber and wished I hadn't bothered. The tide was out and it was a mile and a quarter of dull, brown flatness with desolate, muddy banks and no redeeming features.

I toyed briefly with the notion of cycling back to cross and re-cross the Humber Bridge, only six miles away as the crow flies but a quick look at the map revealed the true implications. Twice through the edge of Kingston-upon-Hull and fifteen road miles. Well,... perhaps not. (I did eventually cycle over the bridge twenty months later, en-route from Yorkshire to Cornwall).

I groped my way out of Brough, which is primarily a light industrial suburb of Hull, and up to South Cave where I was mightily relieved to rejoin the pink line more or less on schedule. Of course this fortuitous resumption of the planned route negated the whole business of the road atlas. I could now jettison page 108 unused. Sorry, environment. Sorry, precious funds. I was just forty five miles north of South Kyme as the aforementioned crow flies but in a different world. The accents were unmistakeably Yorkshire (for a very good reason!) and there were hills. I passed an estate agents sign outside a house which was for sale through Beercock, Wiles and Wick – pure Yorkshire; pure Charles Dickens and almost Monty Python.

A huge bank of cloud was looming up from behind and to my left, maybe ten miles away, and threatening to spoil my afternoon. If nothing else, it was an incentive to get my head down and cover some distance in a hurry. It looked as if I'd be okay.

Passing Wolds Prison I cast my mind back to the previous afternoon, most of which was spent alone in a room with a nice view from the window, a television, tea-making facilities and a bathroom with shower. That had been lonely and depressing enough – what must life be like in a prison cell? Best to be a good boy and not find out.

Heavy rain was now visible off to my left and I was keen to reach a right turn further along my route which would put it behind me again. The cloud crept closer but then came the sharp right bend which left me riding parallel to the direction of travel of the cloudbank. I was batting along at 18 mph and could sense my late father sitting on my shoulder saying "Go on, Boy!"

Then, an hour after stepping off the train into glorious sunshine, the first spots of rain. Three minutes later I accepted the inevitable and stopped under a large tree to don my waterproofs. The wind was lashing around in all directions. This was the first ever use of the waterproofs which I'd bought for my Lowestoft – Land's End ride and hadn't needed.

After a hectic few miles on a busy road with my back light flashing away behind me, the rain became torrential so I sought shelter in the porch of North Cliffe village hall, which was nicely out of the wind. I dug out my all butter shortbread and devoured several fingers. All that was missing was a cup of tea. When the rain eased I set off out of the village hall car park, through a deep puddle and back onto the road. Immediately both wheels started making a dreadful graunching noise. Investigation showed that the puddle had been loaded with some sort of sharp grit which had coated both wheel rims and was now becoming trapped under the brake blocks. I realised straight away that this was not a quick fix job and retreated back to the village hall porch to investigate.

To put things right I had to partially dismantle the brakes which then developed a mind of their own and didn't want to go back in their proper position or to their normal state of quiet efficiency, showing signs of a residue of grit embedded in the brake blocks. Twenty frustrating minutes later I was ready to resume the journey. Happily, the rain had moved on so, to be safe, I carried the bike to the road's edge and off we went again. My brakes weren't right but were as good as I could get them for now.

Nearly all the country roads I'd used on this ride had been dotted with grain from passing trailers bringing in the harvest. I remembered seeing the same thing a year earlier on the way to Land's End. While the percentage loss to the farmers would be miniscule, the grain would be a boon to the local small wildlife.

All too soon I found another huge shower cloud stalking me on the run-in to my night stop at Pocklington. The road turned sharp left to run directly towards the cloud for a mile or so before resuming its former course and I found myself in the bizarre situation of racing towards the shower in order to escape it!

Back on my northerly heading and approaching Pocklington I was congratulating myself on maintaining 15 mph when it dawned on me that this was four minute mile speed and that Dr Roger Bannister and many runners since have averaged this speed on foot for a mile. Humbling. (And top sprinters achieve more than double this over a hundred metres).

I reached the Feathers Hotel in the dry and once the bike was secure in their bottle store, found my room and ran myself a bath. The room was in a separate block behind the hotel, so it was lovely and quiet. While the bath was running I brewed some tea to enjoy as I soaked. I was just about to climb into the bath when there was a huge rumble of thunder. The shower had evolved into a storm and was expressing its chagrin at having failed to catch up with me on the road. I sank into the hot water and enjoyed two cups of tea and three complimentary bourbon biscuits (crumbs in the chest hair – who cares).

Before dinner I went into the bar and supped a pint of Leper Squint bitter from the Abbey Bells Brewery. Strange name; nice pint. So much so that I had a second one with my dinner of Wensley apple and soft cheese pâté followed by steak and ale pie. Sadly, both brewery and ale have since vanished from the landscape. Back in the room I hung up various bits of washing which had now stopped dripping and sat down with a cup of hot chocolate to write up the journal. Everything was back in place and I was on track once more.

Trip mileage:   33.1          Total: 189

*"The wish to travel seems to me characteristically human: the desire to move, to satisfy your curiosity or ease your fears, to change the circumstances of your life, to be a stranger, to make a friend, to experience an exotic landscape, to risk the unknown…"*

*Paul Theroux*

Wednesday 3<sup>rd</sup> September.

## Racing the Rain.

I slept really well – as a result of the return to normality I suppose – and woke at 7.15 to find the washing still very damp. I hunted around for a hair dryer but all of the drawers were empty. Ever resourceful, I used my technical knowledge to fire up the room's individual boiler and laid everything on the hot radiators before going to breakfast. When I returned they were dry enough to be packed and *then* I noticed the permanently wired hair dryer hanging on the wall above the dressing table! I had sat at that table the previous evening to write my journal. Well at least I remembered to shut down the boiler before leaving.

On the road by 9.20 I hightailed it out of Pocklington, pointed the front wheel north-west and set about the task in hand. The weather forecast was not good and I figured that every mile ridden in the dry was one less to be covered in the wet. I had always wanted to visit Stamford Bridge, site of Harold Godwinson's victory over Harald Hardrada, King of Norway in 1066.

Harald: "What will you give me this day?"

Harold: "Six feet of English soil, or a little
more as you are tall above the average".

And so it transpired. Harald was killed and his army defeated, giving Harold a magnificent victory. He then marched his army rapidly south to Hastings where he in turn was killed, leaving the country to William of Normandy.

Despite my lifelong ambition to explore this historical place, personal comfort over-rode opportunity and when I got there, I roared straight through, pausing only for a red traffic light at the modern bridge. In the first hour I covered 13.3 miles. My route was taking me in a large curve round the top of York, heading west then south-west into the wind. Nevertheless the growing cumulus clouds were a tremendous incentive to maintain rapid progress. I didn't take any photos because of poor light, the need for speed and the lack of interesting subjects.

In better light and with less pressure to crack on, Flaxton would have justified a stop. Obviously a prosperous village, it stretched along either side of the road and had a well preserved village pond and various historic artefacts including what may have been another wheelwright's oven. Looking at the properties either side of the road, I should imagine that the well-to-do managers of businesses in the City of York live there. I caught myself doing something which would become a habit over the next few days – checking that my new wallet was still in the handlebar bag. Then on the road in front of me I saw either two weasels or one weasel twice. They are such nippy little creatures it was impossible to be sure. Reaching the edge of a map page I stopped to do the routine changeover and was delighted to discover that Dalton, my next overnight stop, was on the new page. At an average of an hour per page, this meant that I didn't have too long to go.

Off to the south-west (and therefore upwind and coming my way) were some really big cumulus which would obviously be drenching someone soon. They were still around ten miles distant and so no immediate threat. A few miles away and ahead to my right was Kilburn White Horse, carved onto the side of Sutton Bank. As my route had a constant curve to the right the horse didn't gradually drop behind me as it should have done but gradually drew closer or, rather, I drew closer to it. Most disconcerting. A turn-off to the right took me onto National Cycle Route 65 which would carry me the last five or six miles to Dalton. Happily, the right turn put the wind straight on my back and the road began a gentle descent. Suddenly I could freewheel for a few minutes. The clouds continued to grow – and grow nearer – but I was on a roll and on the home run. A soaring buzzard reminded me of Herefordshire.

Far off to the north I could see the misty shape of some serious hills. I had no idea where or what they were. I just hoped they weren't where I was going. In due course I reached the outskirts of Dalton and started to look out for the Jolly Farmer Inn. I was looking forward to a pint of ale as my reward for covering 39.3 miles in the past three hours and ten minutes. I found the pub at the far end of the village, coasted in and parked the bike. It took me several seconds to register the fact that the pub was closed. A sign on the door confirmed that it didn't open on Monday, Tuesday or Wednesday lunchtimes. Damn! I had passed another pub on the way into the village but it hadn't looked at all appealing.

The only other available source of food was the village post office which, technically, was closed but the proprietor was outside, doing a spot of decorating. He kindly sold me a couple of Pepperami sausages, a chocolate bar and a bottle of Orangina which I consumed on a nearby bench seat in an unexpected splash of sunshine.

A solid wall of cloud was marching towards Dalton and as soon as it blotted out the sun I started scouting for somewhere to shelter from the inevitable rain. I hoped the parish church might be unlocked so I headed that way. When I looked, the church door was actually wide open so I took that as an invitation and pushed the bike up the path to the porch. Nobody was inside and it quickly became clear that the open door was an attempt to ease serious problems with damp in the structure of the building. Rugs were rolled back to expose wet floor boards. The first heavy spatters of rain spurred me to action and I wheeled the bike into the porch and ensconced myself on a pew in the dry end of the church with my voice recorder, journal and chocolate bar. I could feel the temperature drop with the rain.

I put my long-sleeved sweater back on and began to write up the day so far. Sitting still after the morning's vigorous exercise my body temperature continued to drop and I paused to change into my long trousers. A sudden noise from the tower made me think I had company and then I was startled by two loud chimes from the church clock echoing around the building. It was two o'clock and that first noise was the chiming mechanism starting up.

I resumed alternately listening to the recorder and writing in the journal but before long I had to stop again to extract my body warmer from the saddlebag and add it to the growing layers of insulation. I phoned the pub but got their answering machine and so continued listening and writing.

The clock struck three and I tried the pub again. This time there was a reply and within a few minutes I was back at the Jolly Farmer meeting landlord Tim a rather disorganised soul. We agreed to stashthe bike in his lock-up and I enjoyed a cup of hot chocolate in the bar while he and his wife prepared my room.

Once I had established myself in the room, which was across the yard from the main building, I set about cleaning several chain oil marks from my trousers. The previous day a dry-cleaning shop had advised me to use Fairy Liquid (other washing up liquids are available) so, in the absence of that, I tried shower gel, which worked amazingly well. I dried the trousers on the room's portable heater and went over to the bar for lasagne, chips, salad and a pint.

On the wall above the bar were five pictorial plates from a set of eight. At home I had five plates from the same set, including the three which were missing from the pub's set. As mine were stored away and doing nothing I told Tim I'd send him the three needed to complete his set when I arrived home. Before retiring to my room for the night I settled the bill in order to be able to leave early the following morning.

Back in the room I swapped texts with Sue and completed the day's entry in the journal. In the room was all that I needed for breakfast and as the weather forecast sounded pretty desperate, I prepared everything for an early departure.

Trip mileage:  40.6       Total:  229

*"The very basic core of a man's living spirit is his passion for adventure. The joy of life comes from our encounters with new experiences, and hence there is no greater joy than to have an endlessly changing horizon, for each day to have a new and different sun."*

*Christopher McCandless*

Thursday 4th September.

# A Long day's Ride.

During the night I hatched a plan to save myself a day's cycling in the rain. A huge area of rain was working its way up the country from the south-west and was due to overtake me the following day. If I leapfrogged that night's stop and rode all the way to the Friday night stop today, I would be able to spend the following day indoors in the dry, watching the rain pass over. It would depend on the room being available a day early and mean cycling around seventy miles in the day but if they could fit me in at the Crown and Crossed Swords at Shotley Bridge, I would give it a go. Never mind give it a go – I'd have to do it or I would be looking for a bed in the wild northern twilight at the end of the day.

Despite an early blue sky over Dalton, the morning weather forecast reinforced the message about storm conditions on Friday so I girded my loins (in shorts!) and went for it. I was away from the Jolly Farmer by 8.20 before the landlord and lady were up, under a sky which had already turned grey. Only four miles up the road I started to feel single spots of rain every now and then. By six miles it was falling steadily enough for me to stop and put on my waterproof top.

The grey light – and the likely distance ahead of me –meant that there was little point in photography and the waterproof meant that I couldn't reach my voice recorder, so my account of most of the rest of the day relies on my memory which, by the time I wrote up the journal in the evening, was already rather blurred.

My original route plan had incorporated quite a big deviation from the direct line to reach my planned Thursday night stop so, taking a gamble on an as yet unconfirmed bed, I was able to skip that deviation and take a short-cut via Scorton and Middleton Tyas, near Scotch Corner. Scorton was a chance discovery from Heaven. The post office there not only enabled me to top up my mobile phone balance (tricky when I had lost the card with my wallet) but also sold me a decent pork pie, some butter shortbread and two energy drinks to fill the bike bottle. It also let me escape the rain for a few minutes.

My journey was frustrating because away to my right and ahead of me the skies were light almost to the point of being blue. Behind me and to my left, over the Pennines, they were dark and depressing. I was cycling along under the front edge of this lot and only ever in light rain. Occasionally I would draw ahead of it and the rain petered out but then I'd have to stop to change maps or fathom a complicated junction and the rain would catch up with me again. On one occasion I was sufficiently confident to stop to take off my waterproof. I didn't even have time to take it right off.

Barton, already beyond my planned overnight stop, was particularly confusing so I sought advice from a lady pedestrian who gave me very convoluted directions which didn't fit what was shown on my map. I asked another lady who tried to send me two miles out of my way via a motorway junction. However, when I explained my way of doing things, i.e. shortest route, trying to avoid traffic, and showed her on my map, she pointed me the right way.

The rain caught up again as I crossed the A1(M), then, half a mile from Barton, I found a strong mobile signal and stopped under some horse chestnut trees to phone around and re-arrange my accommodation. A group of cows in the adjoining field eyed me and my bright yellow waterproof warily. Burning my boats, I phoned my previously intended stop first, told them a hard luck story and cancelled my room. Then I phoned the Crown and Crossed Swords to make sure that I'd have room a night early if I managed to reach them. I explained my predicament and my plan and the landlady said "Of course you'll do it, Pet". Well I'd have to now......

Mileage so far was thirty, with forty or so to go. Say it quickly and it sounds easy. I munched a couple of shortbread biscuits, took a slurp from the bottle and hit the road once more. After a further half mile I joined a Roman road, the B6275, which I would follow in a straight line, due north, for next ten miles. I crossed the River Tees at Piercebridge and three miles up the road I passed out of North Yorkshire and into County Durham. Here I made an exception and stopped to photograph the county sign. The top photo shows the road disappearing up a hill in the background. That hill was the first – and smallest – of many. County Durham was going to make me work for my supper.

*The road – and the first of many hills – ahead.*

*...and intrepid cyclists!*

After a two hundred yard acquaintance with the A68 I turned due east, leaving the Roman road at the top of a particularly steep hill to plunge down through High West Thickley. I only know this from the map because it was a white-knuckle blur of wet, fast bends which did provide a minute's relief for my leg muscles.

I was now in Sedgefield Constituency but saw no sign of our former Prime Minister or his lady wife. To be honest, it probably wasn't their sort of weather. Shildon, where I would like to have visited the Locomotion Railway Museum, was a navigational nightmare. It looked easy on the map but the road planners had been at work and I knew I'd gone wrong when I found myself heading south. That way lay Lowestoft, not to mention the foul weather which I was trying to escape. An elderly gent gave me directions via Bishop Auckland and the A688. A second gentleman said "Orver the bank, round the corner and oop by the King Willy". Eventually a guy who looked and sounded like actor Jimmy Nail, working by the roadside and wearing a matching shade of dayglow yellow to myself said "There's easier ways to get there, y'nar!" when I told him where I was going. He then gave me clear, concise directions which did indeed take me past the "King Willy" – the William IV pub.

Five miles over the hill, at Kirk Merrington, I spotted a seat set back from the road under some trees and stopped for lunch. The pork pie was every bit as good as I had hoped and was followed by two shortbread biscuits. Mileage so far was 54.6 and I dared to take off the waterproof before setting off again. My lunch break was all of ten minutes – it was too cold and damp to linger longer.

Outside Spennymoor I crossed the A688 and was very grateful for the cycle ways which segregated me from the heavy traffic on the junction. Here the traffic planners had got it right. Then a long climb through Tudhoe took me onto the A167 for a while to Sunderland Bridge – presumably the old county boundary – which carried me across the River Wear. More uphill: I looked up at a slow-moving freight train crossing a viaduct high above me and within half a mile was crossing the railway line and looking down on it. The balance was shifting from up and down to mainly up. I climbed up to Brandon, I climbed through Brandon and I continued to climb the on other side of Brandon.

*The view beyond the road, from my lunchtime seat.*

*Durham Cathedral, around three miles away, rises above the city.*

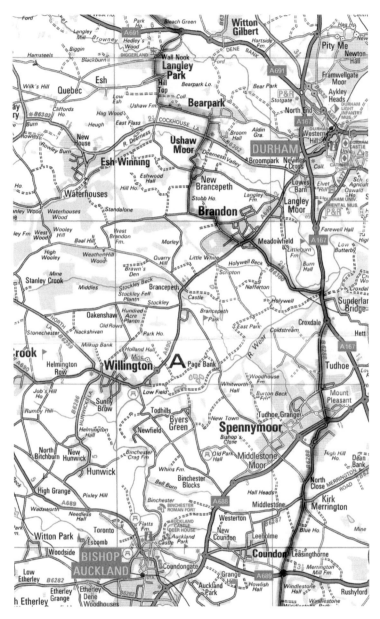

*A sample map page. The "pink line" showed up more clearly on the original.*
*Also, printed on A4 paper, the original was twice this size*

On the road out of Brandon an old gent in a Nissan Micra took a long, hesitant time overtaking me, much to the frustration of following motorists as well as myself. It was distracting having him dithering behind me as I flogged up the hill but eventually he did it. Approaching the top I turned north again and then, after a mile or so, came the inevitable plummet into the next valley. It was a good road with sweeping bends which allowed me to freewheel and rest for a moment as well as making up some time at a fair speed. So fair in fact that, after a mile and a half, I caught up with the old gent in the Micra who then managed to hamper *my* progress. When he saw me in his mirror, looking for an opportunity to overtake, he was - presumably - embarrassed enough to put on a few more mph and stay out of my way.

This was the Deerness Valley which, inevitably, was followed by yet another hill, taking me slowly through Bear Park and on up to the aptly named Hill Top before I dropped into Langley Park to cross the River Browney. When my mileage for the day matched my age - 63½ - I stopped for a snack, sitting on a fence in a brief spell of sunshine, just short of the inspiringly named Stand Against All. I stayed there for ten or fifteen minutes and took a couple of photos before re-mounting and resuming the struggle.

South-west of me – and therefore upwind – cumulonimbus clouds were building and in one or two places the view was blotted out by heavy showers. I began to have a feeling of inevitability but all I could do was to plod wearily on. By now I was walking up the steepest hills. At the top of one hill, the first spots of rain began to fall. At least the decision was a simple one – I didn't need to wait and see what was going to happen – I put on the waterproof. Within half mile the rain was hard enough for me to seek shelter under a tree. After a few minutes the tree started leaking rain onto me so, at the first hint of a lull, I got back on the bike and headed rapidly north-west. Passing Burnhope I saw a magnificent mining memorial built from a colliery winding wheel and a pair of mine railway trolleys but there was no question of a photo.

On the approach to Maiden Law the heavens opened and it fell down in bucketfuls, leaving me to search frantically for shelter. Unbelievably, entering the village, an old man in some sort of transparent smock was up a ladder working on a glassless first floor window as if nothing was happening. What a stalwart.

*A rare splash of sunshine...*

*...and half an hour later a downpour.*

I spotted a bus shelter and was in there, bike and all, before you could say Jack Robinson. It was at least a chance to sit down. With lots of passing traffic, I had to watch out for incoming splashes. This was the rivers-down-the-road, drains-can't-cope sort of rain which kept me trapped (and resting) for fifteen minutes. Once it eased off I hauled myself back on the bike and carried on up the road. By now my legs were shot – level road or downhill: fine but any real uphill reduced me to walking pace. Within the space of a couple of minutes the rain finally stopped and the sun broke through. I glimpsed one end of a rainbow up a side lane. Once more I took off the waterproof and then took some photos of the receding storm clouds and others nearby. I reckoned that I had been caught by a passing cold front.

*Not my cloud but a smaller one passing by.*

A final few undulating miles brought me to Medomsley Edge, above Consett. Then I discovered how much height I'd gained during the day. Still with very dodgy brakes, I started a seemingly unending plunge into the valley of the Derwent (one of three in England) to Shotley Bridge. Each time I thought I'd reached the bottom, I rounded a corner and there was another steep drop. At some point in the upper stages I attained a speed of 42.5 mph.

Suddenly, there was the Crown & Crossed Swords Hotel. I had done it. Coasting to a halt, I checked the handlebar computer – 73.5 miles and the most miles I'd covered in a day since the very early 1990s (and those miles had involved considerably fewer hills). I was too knackered to be elated but I *was* pleased. Three gents were sitting outside the hotel having an early evening drink and were highly impressed when I told them how far I had ridden. To put that in perspective, twice in the mid 1960s I cycled 200 miles, from my home in Buckinghamshire through central London to Margate and back home again, in a day. So the twenty year-old Phil wouldn't have been so impressed with today's effort, though he'd have been pleased to know that his senior self would still be at it 43 years down the line.

The landlady gave me a very warm welcome and let me stash my bike in a kitchen corridor. She showed me around the complex passageways of what had once been two pubs and then left me in my room to make the big decision: beer first or bath? Beer won and I went down and sat in the bar eavesdropping on three Geordies discussing prospects for Newcastle United, where manager Kevin Keegan had just had a bust-up with the board and "discussions are on-going". The ale was a local brew from Wallsend called Geordie Pride and was excellent.

Back in the room, I texted Sue – now on holiday in the Italian sunshine, wise girl – and received her congratulations. Then I got down to the serious business of soaking in a hot bath with a mug of filter coffee at hand. Walking around the room afterwards, I found myself bumping into things and sat down on the sofa. It wouldn't have taken me long to fall asleep there and then, despite the coffee, so I sorted out essentials, did some washing and headed downstairs for dinner and a second pint of Geordie Pride.

I was in bed by 9.20 and asleep by 9.22!


Trip Mileage: 73.5      Total: 303


*"It is not the destination where you end up but the mishaps and memories you create along the way!"*

*Penelope Riley*

*After the storm: the view from my window on the Thursday evening.*

Friday 5th September.

## Rest and Recuperation.

As a result of the early night, I was up and about promptly and squeezed in an hour's exploration of Shotley Bridge before the rain arrived. For what was basically a corner of Consett, it had a lot of history or, more accurately, a lot of information about its history on a series of notice boards. After all, most settlements have their history. The difference was that here, someone had taken the trouble to collate it all and display it for the information of anyone who was interested. (Me!).

As the bulk of the day was to be spent idling in my room, reading and drinking tea and coffee, I shall devote this chapter to the much more interesting subject of the history of Shotley Bridge and the Crown & Crossed Swords. There is documentary evidence that by the 14th Century there was a (water) mill in the village, owned by the Bishop of Durham and the local farmers were obliged, by law, to have their corn ground in this mill. Failure to do so would incur a hefty fine. In the late 17th Century several families from Solingen, in Germany, probably seeking religious freedom, settled here and set up a sword making business. They brought with them the technique of tempering steel, previously unknown in England.

The swords they produced were said to be among the best in the world and were used in the Napoleonic Wars, being particularly noted for the quality of their engraving and gilding. Before the end of the wars sword making gave way to cutlery and farm tools and then manufacturing declined to the point where the families split up and went their separate ways. One family, the Moles, went to Birmingham and set up a sword making business which was later absorbed by Wilkinson Sword. One of Wilkinson's most important modern-day European operations is back in Solingen, in Germany, so completing the circle after three hundred years. In 1799, John Annandale set up two paper mills at Shotley Grove producing fine quality paper. During the 19th Century the business became recognised nationally and in 1895 the combined output of the two Shotley mills reached ninety five tons per week, providing employment for three hundred people. The Annandales also owned a flour making business, sited near the bridge.

The Crown & Crossed Swords, as already touched upon, occupies what were originally two public houses, called The Commercial and The Sword Inn. They were owned by the Oley family, another of the immigrant, sword making families from Solingen. It seems that in the late 18th Century, William Oley was challenged by two sword makers from elsewhere to see who could make the most resilient sword. On the day of the challenge, Oley appeared not to have a sword with him and allowed the other two to demonstrate their swords and boast of their strength. He then took off his top hat and showed them a sword coiled up inside it. The sword could only be removed with the aid of a vice and thus Oley won the bet. Having won the "crown" of sword making in England, the victor changed the name of The Commercial to the Crown and so it was logical when the two establishments were amalgamated into one to call the resulting hotel The Crown & Crossed Swords.

The front edge of the rain arrived so I called into the newsagents to buy some light reading to occupy my day while the rain passed over, exactly as I'd planned. Approaching the hotel, I was surprised and delighted to see an old, two-foot diameter cast-iron badge for the Cyclists Touring Club on the front wall of the building. I don't know when they stopped making those badges but it certainly dated back to the 1950s and could date back to 1887, when they were introduced. Clearly I wasn't the first mad cyclist to have sought shelter at the Crown & Crossed Swords.

*The pub. My window was 1<sup>st</sup> floor, above the blue car.*

*The hotel's emblem and the village centre from my bedroom window.*

*The River Derwent from Shotley Bridge.*

*Brand new houses in traditional style and very tastefully done.*

The rest of the day was spent alternating between my room and the bar, where I lingered over lunch and, five hours later, dinner. I spent a while talking to the room cleaners, two lovely ladies of around forty and fifty, who were probably glad of someone to chat to as a change from each other. They told me some of the gossipy history of the hotel and I gave them a flavour of my journey so far, being grateful for their company.

There was a good, old fashioned, Northern coal fire in a black, cast-iron fireplace at one end of the large bar and most customers, me included, gravitated towards that end of the room, for the psychological comfort as much as for the warmth. Outside, the wind continued to batter the rain against the windows and I congratulated myself on my foresight in beating the worst of it by arriving a day early. And so to bed.

*Not exactly roughing it...*

*The old, rather weather-beaten CTC badge on the hotel wall.*

*The hotel seen from the river. The CTC badge can just be seen between the tops of the white windows.*

Saturday 6<sup>th</sup> September.

# Hadrian's Wall.

The plan had been that I would awake to blue skies, with yesterday's rain clouds disappearing over the horizon. The reality was a tad different: the rain was still there but heavier, the wind was stronger and the sun was conspicuous by its absence. This didn't affect my plans – I had to crack on or forget the whole thing. There were no more free days to wait for the weather to improve.

Clad in my waterproofs, with handlebar bag and saddlebag both lined inside with plastic carrier bags, I left the Crown & Crossed Swords at 10.00 and set off up the road. Very quickly a missed turning put a mile on my journey and a steep hill with a bend at the bottom woke me up to dramatically reduced efficiency of my brakes. I managed to stop, up on the pavement with a foot to spare between me and the low parapet of a bridge, beyond which was a long drop into the engorged River Derwent where, with slower reactions, I would probably have died. My brakes had not been the same since the episode with the grit-laden puddle and now there was the added complication of wet rims and consequently further reduced grip. I made a mental note to be a lot more careful.

Having started at river level I faced the inevitable climb out of the valley. The plus side to this was that, having quickly got chilly emerging into the rain, the work involved in gaining altitude soon generated enough warmth to have me glowing. As I gained height and emerged from the valley, the wind gained strength until it must have been nudging gale force. This was an additional, unwelcome factor because it meant that I was constantly correcting for random gusts which tried to throw me all over the road.

The roads were littered with bits of tree and for a large part of the time I was riding along what amounted to a river. Obviously photographs were out of the question in these conditions so all I had to do was keep the pedals turning, keep my head down, keep gaining height and occasionally do a quick bit of navigation. My target was the Twice Brewed Inn at Once Brewed, up on the Northumberland fells beside Hadrian's Wall – not that far away but far enough in this lot!

Having flogged up onto the tops of the hills, I then dropped right back down to nothing to cross the River Tyne at Bywell. The river was a brown, raging torrent which had already reached the lower branches of trees along its banks. It wasn't far below the road surface on the bridge and was just reaching road level on either side. I imagine the bridge became impassable later that day.

Once over the bridge, guess what – yes, start climbing all over again... Not far into that process I met a girl on a large horse. Like me she was kitted out for the weather and I suppose the horse was waterproof like my bike. We greeted each other, grinned and didn't need to say anything more. Each recognised in the other a kindred spirit who wasn't going to be dictated to by the weather. We also weren't going to stop and pass the time of day.

In some places the force of the water had lifted the tarmac of the road surface and physically shifted it down the road. Having regained height, I was following an undulating course and every plunge into a flooded dip in the road brought the risk that the water may hide a pot-hole or slab of tarmac big enough to send me over the handlebars. The water was gradually finding its way into my shoes – inevitable when they were so close to so much wet road. My journey degenerated into a blur of rain, gusty wind and occasional stops to change soggy map pages. Once I reached the road that runs along the hills parallel to Hadrian's Wall I no longer needed to pay much attention to navigation, I simply followed my nose and kept heading roughly west.

It dawned on me that a few miles to the north and off to my right, the valley was much brighter and staying that way. Frustratingly, the cloud which was dumping endless amounts of rain on me was being boosted by the hills along which I was riding. The cloud was evaporating as it descended into the valley. I really could have done without it.

Crossing the River North Tyne I spotted a whole tree trunk, probably nudging 30' in length, floating towards the bridge on a brown flood of water with standing, white-topped waves. I managed to get out the camera in time to grab a photo after it had shot under me and before it disappeared from view. The last ten miles really dragged and once again several hills reduced me to walking – or rather squelching – on the steeper parts.

*The tree trunk passing rapidly down the swollen North Tyne.*

*The view from my window at the Twice Brewed Inn.*

And so, eventually and inevitably, the Twice Brewed Inn hove into view through the rain-lashed murk. I left the bike against the side of the building and entered the porch. Dry, warm drinkers and diners in the bar watched, more in casual disinterest than in sympathy I felt, as I removed helmet, gloves and waterproofs. On signing in at reception I found that I had been gripping the handlebars in the wet for so long (three hours and twenty minutes with hardly a break) that I had a job to hold the pen to write. In the room I removed my shoes and actually had to tip the water out of them into the hand basin. I was soaked through, partly due to the extreme conditions and partly due to my own perspiration, which had condensed on the inside of the waterproofs. I showered and changed into dry clothes and went down for lunch. The landlord told me later that I was the wettest person to have arrived at the pub in his fifteen years there.

It was good to join the throng in the bar, enjoying the warmth, good company and my escape from the elements. I fell into conversation with a couple who were walking from coast to coast and, like me, staying the night. They told me that they had spent the past three days walking along a few yards apart and, like me, looking at nothing and not talking but simply enduring. The guy said that this was supposed to be their holiday and that, realising the insanity of it, they were going to cut it short and make for the nearest railway station and go home.

Eventually I dragged myself away from the bar to go back to the room to try and get everything dry for the next day. The barman had kindly supplied me with an old newspaper to stuff my shoes and soon the whole room was littered with wet or damp clothes hanging from every available point. I ventured briefly outside to secure my bike in the cycle shed. Then, after a good dinner and a chat over a pint with the young couple back in that warm bar, I staggered up to my bed for a well-earned early kip.

Trip mileage: 33.5     Total: 337

*"If you keep going you'll get there.*
*If you don't, you won't"*

(Me).

Sunday 7th September.

## Plan B.

Although still raining lightly, it looked a little brighter in the morning and the wind had eased. After breakfast I packed everything – most of it nearly dry – and went out to the bike shed. By then the rain had stopped and the sky was trying to brighten so I decided to attempt to improve the efficiency of my brakes. I spent half an hour or so fiddling, tweaking and digging out fragments of grit. I hoped I had done some good but only time would tell.

*My friends departing. The sheep are on Hadrian's Wall and the Roman road.*

The sun had disappeared when I set off along the road west and a gust of wind heralded the return of the rain! As I donned my waterproof I pondered my options. A test of the brakes on the first, steep down-slope showed that my efforts had achieved very little and the next couple of miles confirmed my fears. It was time to reach a decision. I was approaching the Scottish border – crunch point – beyond there my route was along the north side of the Moray Firth and effectively out into the wilderness. Within two days I would be a long way from cycle shops for parts and railway stations for escape back to civilisation.

A road junction with a sign to Haltwhistle seduced me into the painful but sensible decision to call it quits, head for home and re-group. The map showed a railway station there, on the line to Carlisle, so all I had to do was nurse the brakes gingerly down a mile of steep hill into the valley. Then it was half a mile through the town to Haltwhistle station… where I found that there was no Sunday service! Not a problem. It was a little over twenty miles to Carlisle with no steep hills and down here in the valley the rain was lighter. I had to adjust to being on main roads amongst traffic again but on the plus side, the road surfaces were better and no navigation was necessary. It only took me a couple of hours to cover the 24 miles against the wind to Carlisle railway station.

This being a Sunday, there were engineering works – the curse of the weekend train traveller – and the trains were working to a special timetable of which no-one seemed to have a copy. The advice was to keep watching the departure screens and see what turned up. I bought a ticket, a book to read and some bits and pieces for lunch, found a seat and kept one eye on the departure screens (as well as the comings and goings on the station).

Over an hour later a train going via Birmingham was announced and duly arrived. The train was very crowded, with people standing in the gangways, so I took advantage of the weekend special offer of a cheap upgrade to First Class to escape the masses. Within an hour of departure, the situation in the crowded carriages became impossible and the conductor announced that in the interests of safety, First Class was open to all passengers and so, within minutes, they poured in. Fortunately, my carriage was well up the train and so never filled up completely. There was no refund for those of us who had paid for the privilege.

Somewhere on the way south we ran out of the back edge of the rain but it remained dull and grey the whole way. For some reason we stopped in Stafford Station for nearly a quarter of an hour, which was to have frustrating consequences for the rest of my journey. The plan was to alight at Birmingham and catch a train from there to Ledbury but having heaved the bike and my gear onto the Birmingham platform, I found that the delay at Stafford meant that I had just missed the Ledbury train and there was an hour and a half to wait for the next one.

The thought of bumming around dreary, drafty Birmingham New Street Station on a Sunday evening, with the realistic possibility of the Ledbury train being cancelled was too depressing for words. The express was still on the platform and so I scooted down to the lady guard and asked if it called at Cheltenham. She confirmed this but said there were no bike spaces. I confronted her with the fact that I'd just removed my bike from the train, upon which – and with platform staff blowing whistles down the platform at her – she grudgingly allowed me back on.

Even better was the discovery that the train also called at Gloucester, eighteen miles from home compared with Cheltenham's twenty four. My plan ran out at this point since, by the time I exited Gloucester station, daylight was beginning to fade. Fortunately I was able to contact Richard, the Wellington Heath taxi driver whose taxi would comfortably accommodate me and the bike. I agreed to meet him at Maisemore, on the River Severn north-west of Gloucester and about the same travelling time away for each of us. Using the last of the daylight and with my back lamp flashing for all it was worth I rode out of the city, across the A40 and along the side of the Severn to Maisemore. By the time Richard arrived I had prepared the bike to fit into his taxi and within half an hour I was back at home in an empty house – Sue was still in Italy –containing all of my immediate needs: a washing machine, fresh dry clothes, a bath and a bed.

I felt a strange mix of relief at being dry, being able to relax without having to work out the next move of a contingency plan and a sense of anti-climax and defeat, having failed to complete the task at hand. For the moment I concentrated on being relieved, sorting crumpled clothes into the washing machine and sinking into a hot bath with a cup of hot chocolate. Over the next few days, as I got in touch with my sponsors and described the sequence of events the majority of them congratulated me on making the right decision. All of them paid me their sponsorship money on the strength of my promise to go north the following year to complete the job. I had to replace all four brake blocks and smooth the gouged wheel rims with emery and steel wool. The first time I rode the bike after doing that, I applied the newly restored brakes and nearly went over the handlebars.

Trip: 27.7          Total:  365

# Part 2

Now, Where Was I?

Friday 4<sup>th</sup> September.

## Unfinished Business.

A year minus two days after taking the sensible option of abandoning my trip to Ardnamurchan Point and heading for Carlisle and the train home, I got another train back to Carlisle. This time, rather than gales and lashing rain, I set out under a blue sky with fluffs of cumulus and I was eager to pick up the journey where I'd left off. I had an easier start than in previous years as I would pick up the northbound train from Birmingham, 50 miles away, rather than London, 140 miles away.

The train journey was faultless but tedious – I was filled with the nervous energy of anticipation and didn't particularly enjoy the five cramped hours it took to travel from Ledbury to Carlisle, especially as the blue sky gradually gave way to total cloud cover, with a few showers wetting the window to emphasise the point.

It was 2.00 pm when I emerged stiffly onto the platform at Carlisle with all of my clutter. I decided against changing into my cycling shorts, partly because it was fairly cool but mainly because I couldn't face the faff of changing clothes in a toilet cubicle. I assembled the clutter – saddlebag, handlebar bag, helmet, drinking bottle and bike – into a cohesive unit, sat on top of it and pedalled off up the road. It was ten past two.

A little prior knowledge enabled me to short-cut through a pedestrianised area to save the hassle of the city's one-way system on a busy Friday afternoon. But then, too cocky by half, I ignored the strong hint offered by Scotch Street and took off down Castle Street, consequently finding myself heading out of town in completely the wrong direction. Logically, Castle Street led me past the castle and I had a nice view of it over the cricket ground, which was very green after a great deal of rain. Realising my error, I sought advice from a friendly local (who says men never ask the way?) and was soon back on the right road, crossing the River Eden to join National Cycle Route N° 7. This would take me all of the way to the Scottish border at Gretna Green, avoiding the main road with all of its traffic, noise and pollution, and then on to my first night's stay.

As I turned onto the cycleway to follow the north bank of the Eden, out to the west and ahead of me, the sky was brightening. Behind me heavy dark clouds moved east, away from me and towards northeast England and eastern Scotland, which were suffering a repeat of the weather which had defeated me and devastated the town of Morpeth a year earlier. There were large amounts of standing water all over the place so my timing had been impeccable – or, more accurately, fluky – narrowly avoiding what must have been a horrendous morning. I discovered later that they had endured a week of foul weather so my timing had indeed been impeccable, as well as incredibly lucky.

Reaching an unsigned T-junction I made the wrong choice but, almost at once, met two charming ladies who were loading all manner of household things into a Landrover Discovery which they'd parked quite casually in the middle of the lane outside their cottage. I asked directions (again...!) and they pointed me back the way I'd come and across the T-junction, meaning that I had only added half a mile to my journey.

With four miles on the clock I caught my first glimpse of Scotland ahead of me. My route was now taking me beside the West Coast Main Line along which my train had continued its journey to Glasgow. I passed the BSW sawmill at Kingmoor, where (if you believe their website) they convert 305,000 cubic metres of tree trunks to 178,000 cubic metres of planks every year. A very extensive railway yard alongside the sawmill indicated that most of those planks reach the building trade by train. I wonder what happens to the 127,000 cubic meters per year of left over wood and bark. Shredded for gardeners, I guess.

Soon I started getting watery glimpses of the sun and patches of blue appeared ahead of me, though occasional spots of rain cautioned me against over-confidence.

Gradually the route drifted further from the railway until, at Rockcliffe, I took a short-cut down the side of the church and past the 25' high sandstone cliff from which the village gets its name, to skirt the north bank of the River Eden once more. A crowd of either house- or sand- martins were swooping to and fro catching up on food stocks after the wet morning. They must have been preparing for their imminent long migration back to Africa.

*My short-cut past Rockcliffe Church....*

*...and the view to the west along the River Eden.*

St Owens

*A Welsh-sounding house sign which caught my eye.*

*The First House in Scotland Marriage Room.*

*The Cumbrian Mountains across the Solway Firth.*

*Approaching Powfoot, still on National Cycle Trail 7.*

*After forty five years, my second view of the moonlit Solway Firth.*

Two miles on from Rockcliffe I had a minute's rest, waiting at a level crossing for a train to pass, before I turned left onto a local road which carried me between the railway, off to one side and the busy motorway on the other, leading me across the River Esk. There were a good many empty livestock transporters heading up the M6 back into Scotland, having delivered Scotch beef to England, presumably. Approaching the border, as well as signposts for the old Gretna Blacksmith's Shop, there were others for the "Gretna Gateway Outlet Village". There's progress for you.

And so at 3.40 I entered Scotland, almost exactly a year later than planned. Turning left at Gretna meant turning west, straight into the teeth of the strong wind which was doing such sterling work ushering away the clouds. That meant harder work but was no bad thing after five hours sitting on my backside on the train.

Taking a photograph of the Cumbrian Mountains across the Solway Firth reminded me that the first time I saw the Firth was by moonlight from the window of a Vickers Vanguard airliner en route from Heathrow to the old Renfrew Airport, which used to serve Glasgow. The year was 1964; my bike was in the cargo hold; I was nineteen; it was my first ever flight and my first visit to Scotland. I was – and still am – proud to have identified it correctly from such a fleeting glimpse.  And it had happened 45 years ago that very week.

Just before 4.30 and approaching Annan the sun finally broke free of the back edge of the cloud sheet and shone in all its glory. The run down to the Powfoot Golf Hotel was a gentle and most welcome freewheel back to sea level. After checking in I was invited to wheel my bike through the hotel lounge to secure storage (just as I had done two years earlier, at the Langport Arms Hotel in Somerset, on the way to Land's End). My room faced south over the firth which was literally just across the road. I spent a long time enjoying the views and watching dog walkers on the beach and the ever-changing patterns of cloud shadows trailing across Cumbria and the sea. After a substantial dinner, I went onto the balcony and watched the Moon rising over the water in the east before retiring to my bed.

Trip mileage:  26.1          Total:  26

Saturday 5<sup>th</sup> September.

# Bird Day.

The previous evening I had been tempted into consuming a huge dinner which fed too much energy into my bloodstream. That meant that it took me forever to go to sleep and even then, for the first few hours, I kept waking up. Finally I fell into the sleep of the dead, waking suddenly to find that it was 8.30 and I was already behind schedule. A quick (small!) breakfast and rapid packing rectified the situation and I was on the road at 9.36 under a grey sky. The met men were forecasting a belt of rain coming in from the west and I planned to ride towards it, beat it to Dumfries and hole up in a café, shop or anywhere dry while it passed over. Half a mile from the hotel, National Cycle Way 7 took me onto the private roads of a vast mobile home park before launching me out onto country roads, which were more noteworthy for the lack of traffic than their surface quality. The sky remained drab and overcast with just the odd bright patch.

In Ruthwell I passed the Savings Bank Museum. The mind boggled at what that might contain – one assumed that it was run by a retired savings bank cashier or manageress (why did I think it would be run by a lady?). I was too keen to beat the rain to Dumfries to stop and see. Later research on the internet revealed that:

*"The original Ruthwell Parish Bank is now home of the Savings Banks Museum. The eighteenth century building houses a collection of early home savings boxes, coins and bank notes from many parts of the world. There are books on the worldwide spread of savings banks. The modest but important archives include documents and letters on the history of savings banks".*  Well!

At Bank End, just under an hour into the journey, I stopped on the bridge over Lochar Water to change to the next map page. A small plot of bright red and pink flowers – the only colour I'd seen so far – cheered a dull morning and merited a photograph. (Well I thought so, anyway). This was where I bade my final farewell to the Solway Firth and turned inland. Leaving the coast meant gaining height but it was such a gentle process that it hardly registered for most of the time.

*Bank End from the Lochar Water bridge.*

*A cheering splash of colour on a dull day.*

A big old crow appeared over a wall on my right, touched down in the road, saw me approaching about twenty feet away and had to convert his second, settling hop into a re-launching hop to escape over the left hand wall before I got to him. He circled round and flew back over me, presumably looking most indignant, though I don't know how you'd tell. This was to be the start of what would become my Day of the Birds.

Three miles of gentle ascent were followed by three more of gentle (but fairly rapid) descent into Dumfries which, being on the River Nith, is more or less back at sea-level. As I entered the town the first spots of rain fell but in fact, over the next couple of hours, it amounted to spasmodic flurries which were enough to see people open their brollies for a while and nothing more. I parked my bike outside the tourist information centre and set off to do "towny" things. Coffee at Costa was followed by a walk along the river to look at the impressive weir and the old Devorgilla Bridge.

I went shopping for iron rations to sustain me on the forthcoming remote country roads and bought a pork pie, a pack of shortbread and some very exotic mixed nuts and dried fruit from Marks & Sparks. I seized the opportunity to acquire a spare pair of reading glasses as I've reached the age when these things vanish without trace and I would be stranded without them when it came to map reading. Finally, I bought a copy of the autobiography of World War One veteran Harry Patch – who had died recently at the age of 108 – to read in the event of being stranded by rain or whatever. ("Whatever" would turn out to be storm at sea, but more of that later).

Dumfries is a strange town which doesn't seem to make the best of itself from a tourism point of view. They make great play of the Burns connection – he is buried there and spent most of his short, 37 year, life in the area. I suspect that his appeal is mainly to his fellow Scots because they are the only ones who can really understand his language or his sentiments. Eventually, having eaten a wholesome M&S chicken salad sandwich and with no sign of a definite change in the weather, I retrieved the bike, donned my body warmer and headed out of town. A mile or two later a mix-up with the road layout put me on the wrong road but early realisation and deft navigation soon had me back on track.

*Devorgilla Bridge (1432) and one end of the long, diagonal weir.*

*The Midsteeple of Dumfries.*

In its time the Midsteeple of Dumfries has served as a toll booth, a prison, the Town Hall and a court house. When I visited, it had recently completed its latest restoration exactly a hundred years after the one mentioned in the Edwardian plaque shown on the next page.

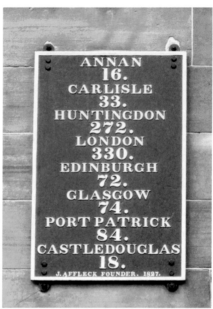

ANNAN
16.
CARLISLE
33.
HUNTINGDON
272.
LONDON
330.
EDINBURGH
72.
GLASGOW
74.
PORT PATRICK
84.
CASTLEDOUGLAS
18.

J. AFFLECK FOUNDER. 1827.

*Why Huntingdon?*

THE MIDSTEEPLE
OF DUMFRIES
ERECTED IN 1707
WAS RESTORED IN 1909
AT THE EXPENSE OF
JAMES H. McGOWAN
OF ELLANGOWAN,
FOR FIFTY YEARS
CHAMBERLAIN OF THE BURGH
1858 – 1908.

A LORE BURNE

South of Newtonairds I crossed from one bank to the other of Cairn Water, the small river whose valley I was following. Before the river bridge was an ancient railway bridge with cast iron panels bearing the cross of St Andrew, the only evidence that a railway had ever passed that way. In contrast to the previous day I was surrounded by clouds in varying shades of light grey but every now and then a little splash of watery sunshine seemed to say "Don't despair". The afternoon's roads were turning out to be of much better quality than those of the morning, even the tiny back roads. Twice I spotted lines of swallows on telephone wires, about to set off for Africa, giving an echo of similar sights in Devon two years earlier.

In the middle of the afternoon I had stopped to photograph some drumlins (an unusual geological feature formed during the Ice Age) when I noticed a large area of blue sky approaching from the west. Less than ten minutes later I was cycling in unbroken sunshine. It was a shame that it had taken so long to arrive, as I'd missed out on lots of good photographs due to the dreadful flat light. Within half an hour the sunshine proved to be merely transitory as a bank of large, black clouds marched over the horizon and chased it away across the sky.

Pausing for refreshment and a rest, six miles short of my next overnight stop at Moniaive [Mon-ee-Ive] I saw my first buzzard of the tour and then, not long after that, what I thought was a pair of kestrels. The kestrels turned out to be sparrow hawks, which I watched zotting down hedgerows into the valley at high speed using the old "You scare them up and I'll catch them" ploy. It was all over too quickly for me to catch a photograph. Down the lane a couple of miles and round the corner I realised that I was riding beside the unmistakeable track bed of a single line railway – no doubt the same one that passed under the bridge I'd seen earlier.

Continuing the ornithological theme, farther down the road, I spooked up a heron from a roadside pond. Unlike crows, herons *always* look indignant so there was no problem interpreting what this one thought. Soon I caught a glimpse of Moniaive across the fields to my right – a welcome sight – so a few minutes later I was at the Craigdarroch Hotel. Once I'd stashed the bike in an outbuilding, I was shown to my room which, like the young lady who led the way, was small but perfectly formed.

*Preparing for the long haul south.*

*The drumlins – low hummocks formed by moving glaciers.*

*Why did the chickens cross the road..? To admire the flowers on the other side.*

*Wayside halt.*

The room was indeed small – just 8' x 6'6" plus a separate toilet and shower. There was no seat or dressing table but a wardrobe and large chest of drawers. However, it was all mine and all I needed. I showered and then went to make a cup of tea….

Ah! The kettle was one of those two-cup, half litre ones with a short lead, so short in fact that when the kettle was plugged into the socket, which was at waist height, it couldn't be placed on the chest of drawers or even on the floor! Rather than stand and hold the kettle while it boiled very slowly, I slid the ¼" thick plate glass top cover of the chest of drawers, complete with television, sideways towards the socket until the kettle could just perch on the end of the glass. A well-earned cup of tea. The television picked up no signal at all – hardly surprising in this deep valley – so that was one all on that score since the previous evening's one had worked perfectly. One has to ask why they provide a TV at all. Perhaps the tourist board rating requires one.

Apart from these minor niggles the hotel was very good, with friendly, helpful staff, good ale and good food. After dinner, on the advice of the receptionist, I strolled up the street to find a mobile signal and text Sue – there was no signal at the hotel – from the bridge at the end of the village. More birds: at the waters edge of Daiwhat Water (yes, really) which flowed under the bridge, a pair of dippers dashed about pecking something from the water. Having texted Sue I walked up the fiendishly steep lane beyond the bridge – designated a cycleway by some unfeeling planner – and looked back over the village. Moniaive, as mentioned, is beautifully located in a meeting of valleys; very like parts of Devon but with different architecture. Even in the half-light I would have taken some photos had the camera not been back in the hotel room.

Trip: 34.8        Total: 60

*"Fare well we call to hearth and hall*
*Though wind may blow and rain may fall*
*We must away ere break of day*
*Over the wood and mountain tall"*
*J R R Tolkien*

Sunday 6<sup>th</sup> September.

## Mamba and Steam.

I had a nervy, unsettling start to the day when I picked up the handlebar bag and all of my single map pages fell out from the map holder onto the floor. It took several minutes to sort them back into order and discover that for the second time on this trip one page had gone missing. Impossible, I hear you cry. Well, I looked under the bed, couldn't see it and so lifted the bed to be sure. I conducted a thorough search of the entire room, including moving and tilting the wardrobe, but nothing. Fortunately it didn't matter that much because it was the second sheet of the day's ride, which I could remember from the planning stage – a simple, straightforward road. It's just that I hate being outwitted by inanimate objects.

Of course, once I'd had breakfast and started cycling the body chemistry balanced up and everything looked brighter. But only for the first four miles. Then what had been a gentle incline became a proper hill, just as it started to spot with rain. Passing through a wooded stretch, I emerged over a cattle grid onto open moorland which was decidedly bleak in the grey light.

With 6.2 miles on the clock I crested the hill to see a sweeping stretch of downhill spoiled only by a pair of cows standing in the road. For some reason they saw me as a threat and took off down the road in their own mini-stampede. I had the speed to pass them easily but a) they might have me off the bike and b) I might spook them into doing something to harm themselves. They kept up a good pace and even from a safe distance behind them I could hear their hooves drumming on the road. Eventually one and then the other found a safe exit onto the moor, leaving me a clear run. Or so I thought – round the next corner I found a dozen sheep wandering across the road. Happily, they quickly spotted me coming and scattered out of my way.

With the prospect of a long run downhill, into the wind I stopped to put on my lightweight body warmer. I decided that the spotting rain didn't justify waterproofs but just thirty seconds on the move changed my mind so I stopped again and put on not only the yellow jacket but the leggings to protect my trousers.

*First sight of real mountains – note the clever way my route veers to the left to avoid them!*

*Entering Ayrshire – and beginning the cross country course.*

Exactly a year before I had been wearing those same waterproofs while battling through gales and torrential rain up onto the Northumberland fells towards Hadrian's Wall and the Twice Brewed Inn. Suddenly, remembering that, this morning's grey skies and light rain didn't seem so bad.

I set off down the road, soon achieving a decent speed for the first time since leaving Moniaive. I couldn't give the bike full head because of the risk of more livestock on the road but it was good to be putting a few miles behind me as I reaped the reward of my earlier efforts. Another hazard was the occasional cattle grid. Spotting one ahead of me and travelling at a little over 20 mph, I was relived to successfully guide my wheels onto a 2" wide wet metal strip across the grid, avoiding a battering from the girders.

The country through which I was riding was what comedian Billy Connolly once christened "MAMBA" – Miles And Miles of Bugger All. It wasn't unpleasant: it just wasn't anything much at all. Away to my right at one point was a wind farm and the tops of the turbine blades were lost in the low cloud. Shards of bark on the road were evidence of the passing of timber trucks, no doubt on their way to Kingmoor sawmill. Looking at the amount of forestry within sight it became apparent why Kingmoor yard needed to be so huge.

This was starting to look like the Day of the Animals – a startled hare leapt out onto the road and easily outpaced my 18 mph, running ahead of me for a quarter of a mile before diving off to the left. No sooner had he vanished than a second hare erupted from the other side of the road and accelerated away from me for a similar quarter of a mile or so. They are reputed to be capable of 40 mph when necessary so this had probably been no more than a gentle stretch of the legs for these two. I pressed on and at long last reached the A713, meaning that I had covered the missing map page and was back on *Terra Cognita*. Joining the main road, I was immediately struck by the amount of litter – cans, bottles, boxes, plastic bags, etc – scattered along the side of the road. It's good to know that people take pride in the tidiness of their cars. A shame, though, about the beautiful countryside they come to look at. A car with a registration number from my home county of Herefordshire passed me – ships that pass in the night and all that.

Entering Ayrshire I soon noticed the different policy of the local authority to highway maintenance. As already mentioned, Dumfries & Galloway's roads mostly have good surfaces whereas Ayrshire's stretch of the A713 bore a striking resemblance to a 'C' road in the mountains – a surface of coarse granite chips littered with cracks, patches and potholes. I have to be careful here not to become a road surface bore because it makes such a vast difference to my comfort, progress and safety. A rough surface brings me increased friction and so reduced speed for more effort whilst cracks and potholes along the three feet that I follow at the edge of the road have to be negotiated somehow, if there is any traffic around to stop me pulling out round the hazard.

Reaching Dalmellington, which I had earmarked as a likely source of lunch, I carried straight on through as the previous evening's pasta was still providing all the slow-release energy that I needed. Only a couple of miles farther on, at Waterside, I heard a steam whistle and smelled coal smoke, which was all it took to lure me off the straight and narrow. I discovered the Scottish Industrial Railway Centre, amongst the remains of the old Dunaskin ironworks, an industrial heritage site. (I didn't enquire whether Dunaskin was akin to the English "Dunroamin"). The Ayrshire Railway Preservation Group had recently moved onto the site and were in the early stages of fulfilling ambitious plans which had evolved over several years of waiting for the move. Friendly, welcoming people and filled with enthusiasm, they gave me a ride twice up and down their 600 yard track in a brake van, behind a locomotive which was two years younger than me! The trip took us past a yard filled with piles of smashed railway sleepers – both concrete and wooden – which were left over from the clear-up after a derailment the previous year. Evidently the last few wagons of a coal train on the adjoining Network Rail mineral line had derailed but the locomotive was so powerful that it travelled a further three miles, with the derailed wagons destroying the track, before the driver realised that anything was wrong.

Back at the bike, having looked around their partially completed exhibition, I ate the M&S pork pie which I had bought the previous day, together with one of two shortbread fingers filched from the tea-making kit in my room at the Craigdarroch Hotel. While I had been exploring the railway centre the rain had petered out so that I could dispense with the waterproofs at last.

*Number 1 - an aged (and historically significant) Barclay diesel locomotive.*

*My "Horse and Carriage": a 1947 Barclay with guard's van.*

A few miles up the road it was a relief to leave the A713 and join the B730. In fact, it was a triple relief because apart from escaping the traffic, the surface improved and having turned north-east for a while, the wind was on my back for the first time this trip. All of this made a dramatic improvement to my progress and having only broken journey at the railway centre, I was suddenly close enough to my next night stop to ring ahead and ask if I was okay to arrive early. (It was only a little after two o'clock). Having obtained clearance from the pub, I received a text from Sue. As I wanted to change out of my damp clothes, I replied to say that I would text her that evening and so, twenty minutes later, I was thankfully removing my saddlebag outside the Stair Inn.

Here was another small, single room, though a little larger than the last one and better thought out. A large A4 notice, lying on the bed, warned of the danger of "The Dreaded MIDGIES". It cautioned guests against opening the window after dark with the light on, hinting at a risk of being eaten alive. Once again, no mobile phone signal. I made a pot of tea (so civilised – a pot), spread damp clothing over the available hangers, ate the caramel bar provided, drank two cups of tea and reclined on the bed. I lay there for two hours, through most of which I slept, then ran a bath via apparently gold plated taps. The hot water was very therapeutic for my weary leg muscles.

Dinner was joyful – a melon and mixed berry cocktail followed by roast gigot of Scottish lamb and all accompanied by two pints of delightful Kilwelly Ale. Well... I'd earned it. The chef at the Stair Inn is a star.

I'd attempted to text Sue but once again, a valley location meant no mobile signal. Asking the bar staff where I would find a signal, I was told "At the top of the hill..." Oh joy! "...or you could use the free bar phone." How very civilised. I called Sue and chatted for a few minutes and then returned to the room to write up the journal.

I sat on the very spacious window sill with the window wide open and forgot the journal for twenty minutes as I revelled in the sights and sounds of the local wildlife. Star performers were around sixty rooks who had congregated above the native woodland, the tops of which I could see over an adjoining rooftop. They wheeled and swooped in their inimitable way, all the while calling noisily to each other. Through the middle of all this flew a solitary swallow, probably cursing the rush-hour traffic. Over the course of a few minutes the rooks all settled into the top of one oak tree and fell silent. Then, out of nowhere, a second group of about the same size zoomed in over my head and dropped straight into the same oak tree with no fuss at all.

For a minute or two all was peace and quiet and the swallows started to take over the airspace. Suddenly the rooks started shouting to each other again and the whole lot rose out of the tree and within about five seconds had disappeared over my head to go and roost elsewhere. I'd love to know who makes the decisions and who initiated a mass move like that. Do they have a leader or do they function as a single organism as starlings do?

By now it was too dark to write and so, heeding the advice of the warning notice, I closed the window before turning on the light. No sooner had I closed the window than an owl started hooting – the night shift had taken over.

Trip:  41.5          Total:  102

Monday 7th September.

# Over the sea to Arran.

In the morning I met the proprietor of the Stair Inn, who was very Glaswegian, very "Hail Fellow, well met", but didn't actually get involved in any conversation. It emerged that I was the only resident and he was there purely to provide me with breakfast, which, to be fair, was nicely done.

On the road at 9.40 I was relieved to see quite a few blue patches amongst the remaining clouds and I caught a glimpse of a rainbow west of me – beautiful, but it did mean there was falling rain only about a mile away. A few minutes later the sun broke through one of the gaps, providing an immediate lift to the mood. The first mile and a half was all uphill, meaning a sharp wake-up call to my long-suffering leg muscles. A reminder of Haverhill in 2007 came in the form of airliners coasting overhead with their engines throttled back, en route to Prestwick Airport. As on the previous day, I passed several fields of grain which was clearly past its best but far too wet to be harvested.

The B730 had become a more or less straight, undulating highway. I was sprinkled by one shower, possibly the same one which had given me the rainbow, but otherwise, I was blessed with patchy sunshine and a following wind on my shoulder. After a while I began to notice more houses along the road and it started to feel like commuter land, with tidy bungalows and houses. Then quite suddenly there were several large commercial / industrial units in sight. I was approaching Irvine, the first of a cluster of towns between Kilmarnock and the Firth of Clyde.

At Dreghorn I spotted a sign for National Cycle Way 73 where it crossed over the road I was using. Against my better judgement, I forsook the road and joined the cycle way, which took me into a 1960s housing estate. There were no further signs at all but for the first mile or so the route was pretty self-evident (though "pretty" is not a word I would use to describe the outskirts of Irvine). Then it became impossible to tell which path was the correct choice for NCW73 from several available options. I took to the road again, headed in roughly the right direction and awaited developments.

Developments came in the guise of NCW73 crossing the road in front of me and quite clearly signed. Once again I was seduced by the off-road option and once again – within a quarter of a mile this time – I was confronted with a three-way junction and zero indication of which route was the cycle way. I was about to return to the road when my guardian angel arrived in the form of a friendly local cyclist who offered to guide me through the labyrinth and see me onto the right path. He told me that he hadn't been out on his bike for a fortnight and had been lured out by the sunshine. I followed him around the winding complexities of the system until he could set me on my way over a clearly marked section of the route, which I would never have found on my own. He was quite in awe of what I was doing and wished me bon voyage as we parted. The cycle way was well signed now and led me, traffic free, through the backwaters of Irvine, Kilwinning, Stevenston and into Saltcoats, weaving and doubling back on itself so much that it must have added a couple of miles to my journey. It seemed that the planners didn't care where they took me so long as they protected me from the traffic.

I stopped on the edge of Kilwinning to photograph a statue of Robbie Burns, overlooking the uninspiring River Garnock, and shed two layers of clothing since the sky was virtually clear now. How ironic that I finally had good photographic weather when I was riding through the back yard of nowhere. The only point of real interest was passing the site of the explosives factory at Ardeer where Alfred Nobel – he of the Nobel Peace Prize – developed dynamite in 1865. Dynamite was an alternative to the extremely volatile (and therefore lethal) nitro glycerine, which had been used until then, and was much safer to handle. For obvious reasons the factory had been spread over an extensive and remote tract of sandy wasteland between a river estuary and the sea. Traces of the old buildings and explosives stores were still visible.

With my map on top of the handlebar bag in front of me I should have been aware that I was approaching the Firth of Clyde but it was still startling to gain my first glimpse of the sea when it was only about fifty yards away! I had followed National Cycle Way 73 down a concrete path between two high fences and now rounded a bend to find myself on the scruffy, potholed seafront road with the sea just the other side of a railing.

*Robbie Burns.*

*A fairly boisterous sea and the seafront road leading into Ardrossan.*

This seemed like a good time to take a break to savour this minor landmark in my journey and gaze across the water to the Isle of Arran, where I would be spending the night. There was no mistaking that this was the Atlantic: even behind its screen of islands and the Kintyre peninsular, the air was fresh and the sea was attacking the sea-wall with some gusto. It had a completely different feel to the Channel or North Sea coasts. Trolleying down through Ardrossan to the ferry terminal, I bought tickets for the first two of the five ferries I planned to use and went to find lunch. On the advice of the girl in the ticket office I pedalled back up the road half a mile to the local Asda, where I enjoyed an excellent two course lunch, with a drink, for a fiver. While I was there I bought a couple of small pork pies as emergency rations for the following day, when it was forecast to be wet all day.

I drifted down to the harbour and awaited the arrival of the good ship *Caledonian Isles,* which duly appeared and, despite a fresh wind and choppy sea, was expertly manoeuvred into the tight little dock. I stood at the end of the gangway and watched the incoming passengers disembark, making wild guesses at their journey's purpose and who they were. Pretty soon we outgoing passengers and vehicles were safe on board and the ferry was extracted just as expertly from its shelter to carry us smoothly over to Brodick, on the Isle of Arran. Midway through the crossing I spotted the glistening head of a seal, calmly watching us pass by.

Once back on the bike and on the move my first impression of Arran was – surprise, surprise – the state of the roads. The outer four feet on the edges of the road, where we cyclists live, was a dreadful mix of cracks, potholes, badly fitting drain covers etc, etc. After half an hour it all improved, leaving only one gripe (better to get it off my chest) which was that now there was some scenery to photograph, the sky had clouded over. Then I spotted an old friend – a sign for National Cycle Way 73! It had accompanied me across the water and was going my way as I headed along the north-east shoreline of the island. A pair of seals surfaced for air in a bay as I rode past.

A large cargo vessel was moving down the channel towards the open sea, looking very likely to collide with the *MV Caledonian Isles* as she set off on the return crossing to Ardrossan. Disaster was averted however as the cargo ship gave priority to the ferry.

*MV Caledonian Isles on her way into Ardrossan with Arran in the background.*

*Approaching the jetty at Brodick, Isle of Arran.*

Suddenly I was screeching to a halt and reaching for the camera as I spotted a seal on a rock, well clear of the water, arching its back and looking very photogenic. I had taken the second picture before I realised that this seal must have been the star of a great many similar, rushed photographs because in fact it was a very lifelike, bronze statue! Ah well...

A few miles up the coast, the road dipped and swooped sharply to the right and on the inside of the bend I glimpsed a tiny harbour containing a miniature, replica Viking galley. It had places for ten oarsmen plus the helmsman with the traditional, fearsome dragon's head and tail on the prow and stern respectively. On the opposite side of the road was a partly finished, life-sized, wooden model of a shark, leaning against a shed. Obviously some serious craftsmen lived in the vicinity.

The harbour entrance just accommodated the little ship, making me wonder if it had been built especially. Maybe small fishing vessels once shared its home. Another story I shall never get to know. I once saw a similar – though bigger – replica Viking ship in Lerwick, in the Shetland Islands. That one had been big enough for a crew of thirty and had a concealed engine for days when the wind failed.

Approaching Sannox, the road left the coast and cut diagonally across the northern end of the island to reach Lochranza, where I was to stay that night. My tired legs had a nasty surprise – a long uphill stretch – at the top I rounded a bend to see a further enormous, winding hill on the road some way ahead of me. From a distance I estimated it to be a good half mile long, which turned out to be a slight underestimate as, when I reached it, I measured it at 1.6 miles of steepish climb.

I applied the old maxim that had sustained me in storm-lashed Northumberland a year earlier: "If you keep going, you'll get there. If you don't, you won't". I engaged a very low gear, twiddled the pedals for an age and inevitably bike, bags and I arrived at the summit. Part way up I had the compensation of seeing a pair of golden eagles soaring above the mountains.

Of course, having left a ferry port and being en route to another ferry port, basic physics came into play. What goes up must come down – and it took a fraction of the time. The road descended steeply for a mile and a half around the end of Torr Nead an Eoin, an impressive mountain which is, apparently, popular with eagles and climbers. Well I'd seen the former and could easily understand the latter. I couldn't go too mad because the road was so rough that it had the potential to throw me right off the bike and the ubiquitous sheep were lurking. Even so, my computer told me that at some point during the descent I reached 38.2 mph. Very cooling after a long, hard climb.

As soon as the way levelled out I was into the outskirts of Lochranza village and could see its castle across the marshy estuary of the small (nameless) river which enters the sea at the end of Loch Ranza. I took a few photos, taking advantage of a break in the clouds, and then spotted the ferry from the Mull of Kintyre approaching the jetty at the far end of the village and so went on down there to watch it arrive. Having seen the ferry safely berthed I ventured up the drive towards the castle and as I did so, noticed a red deer grazing near the path, I grabbed the camera and took an insurance shot using the telephoto zoom in case it spooked and ran off. I needn't have worried as it totally ignored several passers-by and simply continued feeding. I eased my way to within about twelve feet of it and, after giving me a quick glance to check me out, it (she!) carried on munching her mixture of grass and nettles.

*Lochranza Castle with the main loch beyond.*

*The trusting doe.*

The Scottish version of English Heritage, Historic Scotland had provided an informative notice detailing the history of the castle. The original building is believed to have been built in the early 13$^{th}$ century by "Sween" who, I would guess, was of Scandinavian descent – Sweyn or Sven? – since the Isle of Arran was nominally Norwegian territory until it was sold to the Scots in 1266. The L-shaped tower which exists today was built in the reign of James VI (1567 – 1625) and is typical of the castles built in that period. The north-eastern corner collapsed in a violent storm in 1897, by which time the castle had been long abandoned.

Back in the 21$^{st}$ century it was time to go and check in to the Lochranza Hotel. Joy of joys – I had a decent sized room and a double bed – space to spread out at last. The TV and shower both functioned perfectly and once I had turned off both radiators (the Scots seem to love hot rooms) everything was good – except the weather forecast for the following day.

Trip: 42.2          Total: 144

*The Lochranza Hotel's own photograph, taken on a brighter day.*
*My room was the one at top right.*

Tuesday 8th September.

## Rain Stops Play.

I had decided that I didn't need to catch the 9.15 ferry as, once on the mainland, it was going to be a straight dash to Oban through foul weather with no reason to linger along the way. Consequently I was relaxed but resigned to a soaking as I went down to breakfast. The waitress shattered my plans by saying that she didn't think that the ferry was running and that quite possibly it wouldn't run at all for the rest of that day. I felt a change of plan coming on.

After breakfast I walked through a damp, grey, breezy morning to the jetty. The ferry was there but an illuminated sign said that there would be no sailings that morning and the situation would be reviewed at 1.00 o'clock. The problem was that in high winds the far jetty, at Claonaig on the Mull of Kintyre, was unsafe for passengers so although the ferry could safely embark us and take us over to the mainland, we couldn't safely disembark when we got there.

As far as I was concerned, that meant there were no sailings for the day. In those weather conditions an afternoon departure didn't leave me enough time to reach Oban reliably by nightfall. (I was to discover something on the following day which meant that I was fortunate not to have tried).

The hotel confirmed that they could accommodate me for a second night so I phoned ahead to Oban and shifted my booking back one night. After that I had planned to spend two nights at Sonachan, on the Ardnamurchan peninsular, so I phoned the Sonachan Hotel to cancel the first night, thus putting myself back on schedule. There was no reply to my call so I left a message on their answer machine explaining my predicament and cancelling the first night's stay.

I returned to my room, dug out the autobiography of First World War veteran Harry Patch which I'd bought in Dumfries and read a couple of chapters. There being no mobile signal in the room I had to go onto the landing to send Sue a text, bringing her up to date. Already it felt strange not to be on the bike.

*The ferry, idling the morning away at Lochranza jetty. Look at that sky!*

*The castle, showing the collapsed north-eastern corner.*

*The deer in their adopted home – four in the front and more in the trees.*

*Seaweed marking the high tide line outside the Lochranza Hotel*

Back in the room I made a cup of coffee and read some more. Realising the opportunity I had, I did some washing and hung it in the bathroom to dry. Out on the landing to communicate with the outside world I watched a huge, dark red squirrel scoot across the front lawn of the hotel. Noticing a break in the rain I ventured outside for some fresh air and discovered a stag and nine does, living in the garden of a ruined house next door but one to the hotel. They were quite nonchalant about my presence and ignored me while I took photographs of them. Every property in the village had eight foot high fencing surrounding it so the deer were obviously permanent residents and always on the lookout for a chance to munch any flowers and vegetables.

The rain resumed its dismal, grey veil and so I retreated to my warm room and Harry Patch. I simply couldn't raise the enthusiasm to put my waterproofs on and properly commit myself to the Great Outdoors. Unable to justify – or manage – a restaurant lunch, I retrieved the two pork pies secreted in my handlebar bag, along with a few fingers of shortbread.

In another break in the rain I went to establish the situation at the ferry. It was missing from the jetty and so had clearly resumed the service. Sure enough there it was, on its way back from Claonaig. When it arrived I got talking to a disembarking cyclist called Gus and we compared notes for ten minutes or so. Yet again though, rain drove me back indoors so by the end of the afternoon I had finished "The Last Fighting Tommy" – an excellent read – and felt wearier than if I had cycled forty miles.

Never was it more truly said of Scotland "If you don't like the weather, wait five minutes and it'll be different". Sitting in the bar enjoying dinner I looked out to see an endless curtain of fine rain drifting down the loch. Literally five minutes later the first sunshine of the day was glancing off the masts of moored sailing boats. Not long after that really heavy rain was lashing down! I settled my bill and went to pack everything away in preparation for an attempt on the 9.15 ferry the following morning.

Trip: 0                    Total: Still 144

Wednesday 9<sup>th</sup> September.

## A Comedy of Errors.

*Morning light.*

*Gulls scatter as the ferry arrives at Lochranza.*

On a lovely, sunny morning I caught the ferry with time to spare. On board I met fellow cyclist Ian who, I discovered later, hails from Basingstoke, close to where I used to live, south of Reading. He had already cycled across Arran from Brodick that morning, including flogging up those formidable hills, to catch this ferry. On his way from Land's End to John O'Groats he was on a different schedule to me (and, to be fair, also about half my age). He was on a sponsored ride for Alzheimer's Disease Research so I popped a donation into his collection box.

Disembarking at Claonaig I noticed a sign saying that Oban was 58 miles away – clearly the signed route went the long way round to avoid the smaller roads of my planned 40 miles. Ian and I started off together but it became apparent, after only a few miles, that I was holding him back. We swapped cameras for a moment to take photographs of each other so that each would have a photograph of himself on the road. We shook hands and agreed to meet later in Oban – he was planning to follow a route that was twenty miles longer and even hillier than mine.

Ian was off up the road like a long dog (my grandfather's expression, the long dog being a greyhound) emphasising my humble rate of progress. He rounded a corner, started up a hill, glanced back and was gone. I, in turn, pottered round the same corner and up the same hill. Looking back I spotted a nice view to the south and stopped to take a photograph. Back on the road – single track with passing places – I noted a large pick-up coming towards me. The hill meant my progress was very slow and there was no passing place where we could cross, so I waved to him to come on and pulled over to the side of the road to give him a free run.

As I came to a halt I stretched my left leg out to put my foot on the verge, only to find that it was just long, deep grass with nothing substantial underneath on which to rest my foot. As my foot continued downwards the bike and I began to list to port and my weight, plus that of my large, heavy saddlebag, pivoting round the back wheel, lifted the front wheel from the ground. As soon as that happened, all was lost. Everything went into slow motion as the inevitable unfolded around me. The list to port turned into a full roll.... descending backwards towards the ditch.

Now this was no neat, manicured Home Counties sort of ditch – this one could have hosted the National Bog-Snorkelling Championships! Tall grass hid peat, mud and orangey-brown water, all of which awaited me and the bike. I found time to think "They're watching this – how embarrassing" as I extricated myself from the bike and turned myself in mid-air so that I would land on my arms and legs astride the water. The bike finished upside down in the ditch behind me. To my approaching audience I must have vanished – quite comically – in an instant.

*My route was actually up this road the other way but the sun dictated this angle.*

*This was taken about three minutes before my off-road excursion.*

Embarrassment lent speed and I quickly scrambled muddily back up to the road as the pick-up came to a halt beside me. Naturally seeing me as some doddering old fart, the first concern of the young couple inside was that I might complicate proceedings by conjuring up a heart attack or a broken hip. The standard opening gambit of "Are you alright?" brought the reply "Very embarrassed, but otherwise fine". I dragged the bike out by its wheels and laid it on the side of the road, at which point it became apparent that the handlebar bag had come open and two thirds of its contents, including my expensive camera, were still in the ditch. Fortunately they had landed on some tufty grass and so the larger items such as camera, mobile phone and wallet – were only partially immersed.

The guy from the pick-up was a star, straddling the ditch and retrieving everything he could find. His lady wife was still concerned about my welfare and asked if I was sure I was okay. If he hadn't been there I might well have suffered a relapse – she was very attractive and a reassuring cuddle wouldn't have gone amiss – but apart from muddy hands, sleeves and lower trouser legs, I had only the embarrassment to contend with. They were both keen to help but there was really nothing more they could do to improve my situation. In retrospect, I guess they appreciated that I was in this predicament because I'd endeavoured to give them an easy passage down the road. I thanked them profusely for their help and let them go on their way.

I needed to clean myself up. My handkerchief lasted about thirty seconds before it was brown, waterlogged and ruined. I needed something else and racked my brains. Inspiration came in the form of a tee shirt which was packed near the top of my saddlebag. I was able to ease it out without opening the bag and proceeded to temporarily ruin that, too, as I cleaned myself and the various pieces of kit from the handlebar bag. The only casualty – and the most expensive to repair – appeared to be my camera, which wasn't working as it should. I cleaned and dried it some more but to no avail so I packed everything back into the bar-bag and got back on the road. Once I was on the move again the breeze started to dry my filthy, brown sleeves and trouser legs. With around forty miles yet to go I needed to make up some time and, preoccupied as I was with how best to sort the camera situation, the next few miles passed quickly and I found myself at Tarbert. I paused to take stock and face an uncomfortable truth.

Every sign that I had passed agreed that there were eighteen more miles than I thought between me and Oban and as the signs had been there longer than me, it had to be assumed that the signs were right. A shopkeeper in Tarbert confirmed this. Oh joy – my day was getting better and better. With more than 50 miles to go I had to hit the road and stop for nothing. The discrepancy in distances dated back to an error made more than eighteen months earlier, when I had been planning the route from Lowestoft to Ardnamurchan Point. I had obviously missed a mileage number (18!) on the road atlas when totting up distances between overnight stops. The underlying cause of that was a difference in scale of the atlas coverage for the Borders area compared with the rest of Scotland.

To avoid the remainder of the journey becoming a photographic non-event, I bought a simple digital camera with a 3X zoom (compared to the 18X zoom of my regular camera) and no eye-level view-finder. Immersion in the ditch had also rendered my voice recorder dead to the world. I had bought new batteries but couldn't afford the time to fiddle about replacing them, so my record of the rest of the day is from memory. My sole priority was to propel my bike and myself northwards, post-haste. The journey is a blur now because all I did was put my head down and pedal. I carefully avoided checking progress for most of the time – I remember seeing a sign some way ahead and thinking "I need that sign to say less than 40 miles to Oban" and, when I reached it, it saying 38.

Much nearer to Oban I found one of those wonderful shops that you only find in rural Scotland which sell everything you could ever want. I bought drinks to top up my bike bottle and a bridie – Scotland's equivalent of a Cornish pasty. The young lady who served me was delightful, sympathetic and full of encouragement. Outside, whilst topping up the bottle, I talked to a fellow cyclist – another "End-to-Ender" – who had already covered 62 miles (my new total for the day) and had a further 60 yet to ride! In the 1960s that would have been me.

I remember slogging up the last big hump on the approaches to Oban and also being held up in a queue at traffic lights on the way into the town centre. I was relieved to spot the Columba Hotel, an imposing old building and easily reached.

The girl on Reception was unfazed by my mud-streaked, weary appearance and soon I was settling in to my third floor room with views across Oban harbour towards Mull. I ran a bath and gratefully sank into it. The time was around six o'clock.

I had arranged to meet Ian, from the morning's ferry, in the bar – he was staying at Oban youth hostel – and so, after doing essential washing of clothes, hanky, etc., I wandered down at around 7.15, bought a pint and sat in a corner to wait for him. He arrived not long after and I bought him a pint too. He was also tired, having covered twenty (hilly) miles more than me, plus 14 on Arran. I had done 61.8 for my sins, so he had done over 95.

Ian bought a second round and by the time we'd finished that, the kitchen had closed for the night, leaving me looking for a meal. When we parted company Ian pointed out a chippy which he'd seen earlier and I headed over to buy a haddock supper from the verrry aRrrussian couple running it. I smuggled the supper back to my room, ate it (it was delicious) and fell into bed without giving it any time to be digested.

Trip: 61.8          Total: 206

*Evening light. Misty Mull and, in front, Kerrera from my room window.*

# Thursday 10<sup>th</sup> September.

## To the Point.

From my window in the Columba Hotel I could see The Isle of Mull dominating the horizon. After crossing the Sound of Mull on the ferry I would spend much of my afternoon riding along its north-east side in order to catch another ferry to Ardnamurchan Head. After checking out, my first port of call was the CalMac ticket office at the ferry terminal to buy tickets for the two ferries. I must mention the excellent value for money of CalMac ferry tickets – I don't know if they are subsidised but each time I went to buy my tickets I was astonished at how little I was charged. Having bought the tickets, I cycled across town to the Co-op supermarket to stock up on the usual rations: shortbread fingers, a couple of pork pies and bottled drinks to fill the bike bottle. I burbled back to the ferry terminal in time to witness the arrival of the ferry and the precision seamanship involved in getting a reasonably large, sea-going vessel up to the slipway. I know they do it many times a day but every time must be at least a little different and – a sure sign of expertise and professionalism – they make it look so easy. There was less skill involved in getting half a dozen wheelie bins off the ferry, up the ramp and onto the dock.

Approaching Craignure on the ferry I religiously took photographs, which must have been identical to literally tens of thousands taken by other ferry passengers over the years, of the very picturesque Duart Castle. The name Duart means "Black Point" in Gaelic, and that is where it sits, dominating the Sound of Mull. The first castle was built here in the 13th century for the MacDougalls. The MacLean's acquired the castle in the late 14th century, and added the tower house. Lachlan, the 11th Chief of the clan MacLean, is remembered as the man who left his wife, Margaret, on the Lady's Rock, hoping she would drown. She was rescued by a fisherman and went back to live with her brother, the Duke of Argyll. Not surprisingly Lachlan was later murdered – in 1527 – by one of Margaret's cousins, Campbell of Cawdor.

In 1588 the Spanish Galleon, Florencion, part of the ill-fated Armada which was trying to get back to Spain the long way round, made landfall here. It was summarily blown up by the MacLeans and the unfortunate crew were thrown into Duart's dungeons.

*Morning. Oban harbour, Kerrera and, in the distance, the Isle of Mull.*

*Yachts moored in Oban harbour from the Mull ferry.*

*Duart Castle, Isle of Mull*

Recently the wreck of a Cromwellian warship, the Swan, which sank in Duart Bay in 1653 has been found under 40 feet of water. It was sent to pound the Royalist MacLean fort, but was sunk in a storm before it could do so. The MacLeans were driven from the castle during the Jacobite rebellion as they were staunch Jacobites, and they retreated to the Treshnish Isles. Government troops then occupied the castle for some years and it was burnt when the garrison left in 1756. Duart remained a ruin until it was bought in 1911 by the 26th Chief, Sir Fitzroy Maclean. A veteran of the Crimean War, Sir Fitzroy was over 70 when he restored the castle. [I once met his successor as Chief, Sir Charles MacLean].

(All historical information courtesy of the *Scotland Calling* website).

Once disembarked at Craignure I lingered for a few minutes while the ferry load of cars and a gaggle of wild, long-haired, noisy motorcyclists roared off onto the island roads. Once peace was restored I set my sights on Tobermory, from where I would sail back to the mainland, in the shape of the Ardnamurchan peninsular. The road for the first few miles was new, smooth tarmac and I began to entertain thoughts of an easy trip to the ferry but then the new surface came to an end and I resumed having to keep one eye on the road to avoid potholes and protuberances as usual. Three micro-lights buzzed over, making the most of a beautiful, sunny day. I paused to photograph a huge orange toadstool and then four greylag geese took off from the foreshore to my right, swung round and flew straight up the road towards me at just above face level, before veering off back over the sea. Then I noticed a solid sheet of cloud, looming up from the west and about to obscure the sun. My brief idyll was over.

I had to crack on because there wasn't much spare time in my schedule between ferries. Though no longer silky smooth, the road was at least level so I was able maintain a decent speed for a good few miles. But then, in the distance, I glimpsed a coach labouring up a long, steep hill which was clearly a continuation of the road I was following. I upped the pace over the last three or four miles of flat road to allow a little more time to flog up that hill. When I reached it I was quickly reduced to a very low gear and not much more than walking speed. As I gained height I caught my first, misty, drizzly sight of Ardnamurchan. It looked a miserable place to be. And it was where I would be – within three hours…

*A 6" diameter toadstool at the roadside.*

*An interested islander.*

*A pair of derelict fishing boats on the foreshore beside the coastal road.*

*The famous coloured houses on Tobermory harbour side.*

Eventually I staggered to the top of the hill and as I prepared to launch myself down into Tobermory, it began to rain. Rapidly, because the minutes were ticking away, I donned my waterproof coat and shot down into the town. I looked in vain for the usual road signs to guide me to the ferry terminal. As a safe bet, I headed along the side of the harbour but though there was a pier, it clearly wasn't what I was looking for. At the far end of the harbour road the problem was solved – the road became a slipway, simply dipping into the water with just a gate to control access.

With ten minutes to spare and no sign of the ferry itself, I grabbed a couple of photographs, in dreadful light, of the harbour front shops. They were the setting for the BBCs "Balamory", a favourite programme of Sue's grandson Elliott. I bought a job lot of twenty postcards of Ardnamurchan Point and lighthouse, ready to trumpet the completion (a year late) of my mission. The little ferry, similar to the Lochranza – Claonaig one of the previous day, duly arrived and within a few minutes we were clearing the headland at the end of the harbour and I took my first proper look at Ardnamurchan. Initially there wasn't much to see as the whole head was shrouded in orographic cloud but happily, as we crossed the water I was able to watch the cloud gradually disperse until, by the time I disembarked at Kilchoan, the hills were cloud-free.

I was on the home straight (though only of my original quest – I now had a further week's journey ahead of me). A huge welcome sign informed any traveller who didn't know that they were on the westernmost headland on the British mainland. I headed inland, following signs for the lighthouse, and within a mile began to climb and then drop, climb again and then drop again, but never dropping as much as I climbed and so steadily gaining height.

A little over three miles from the ferry I spotted the Sonachan Hotel. I popped in to let them know I was around and then carried on towards my goal. Miraculously the sun was now shining out of a largely cloudless sky. All I needed were hordes of trumpeting angels, choreographed by Busby Berkeley, to escort me over the last few miles into the sunset. They failed to materialise so I soldiered on alone.

*Ardnamurchan Head, lost in low cloud.*

*The last wisps of cloud hang on.*

WELCOME
TO
WEST ARDNAMURCHAN

The most westerly point
on the U.K. mainland

There were two or three seriously steep rises as I neared the lighthouse but the adrenalin was flowing and I just charged up them and kept going. I paused to photograph the top of the lighthouse peeping over the hills – my first glimpse – and then rattled off the last half mile, rounded a bend and found myself at... a red traffic light! There was a narrow stretch of road with blind bends so they had installed the westernmost traffic lights on the UK mainland. I waited for them to turn green and jiggled my position to try and trigger the sensors which would register my presence but they stayed stubbornly red. In the end impatience got the better of me and, crossing the lights at red, I wove my way round the empty road and at last up to the lighthouse.

I was there, 31.8 road miles and two sea crossings from Oban. My closest welcome was from a swarm of midges but I shook them off with a fifty yard downhill scoot on the bike. A more distant – and more appreciated – welcome was from an eagle, soaring between the hills. Because of the intervening year it didn't feel like arriving from Lowestoft. Nevertheless it was a good feeling to have fulfilled my dream. I texted Sue, newly arrived (in drizzle and heavy cloud!) on the Greek island of Skiathos and then phoned my son Andy at Bristol. He had to be reminded where Ardnamurchan lighthouse was, and of its significance but when the penny dropped he was delighted for me.

I wandered around the complex of buildings, disappointed that the tower and the visitor centre were closed. I asked a passer-by to take the traditional "Mission Accomplished / Conquering Hero" photograph of me and my trusty bike with the lighthouse in the background and then I hit the road back to the Sonachan Hotel.

Having booked in I was escorted to my room, in a separate building 100 yards away and up a very steep slope. Once I'd carried all of my bags and bits up to the room I decided that the bike would be just fine where it was – down behind the main hotel building. The hotel being on a Scottish headland and surrounded on all sides by peat, the tap water was the colour of weak tea (without milk) but tasted fine to drink. I showered, changed, unfolded my world from the saddlebag and went down to the main hotel for a beer and a chat with some of the regulars, followed by dinner.

Later I set about re-arranging my itinerary so that I would be able to spend a second night at Sonachan after all. I needed to cancel my stay at the Ledgowan Lodge Hotel at Achnasheen. Despite the fact that I was giving them five days' notice of cancellation, they insisted on charging my credit card for a full night's stay. All of the hoteliers who heard about this agreed that it was unreasonable. Apart from anything else, even if they did not re-let the room they were saving on breakfast and laundry.

Trip: 34.7                              Total: 241

Distance cycled from Lowestoft to the Lighthouse was 602 miles.
(It would have been something like 650 without the train ride I took to get back on schedule after losing my wallet in Lincolnshire).

*The road to the lighthouse.*
*This is typical of many of the roads I used in the west of Scotland and better surfaced than many of the main roads to which I occasionally had to resort.*

*Sonachan, with the annexe towering over the other hotel buildings.*

Friday 11th September.

# Ardnamurchan.

The forty eighth anniversary of the day I started working for a living with the Post Office Telephones – later BT – this was my day off from going anywhere special in order to explore locally. In particular I planned an investigation of the caldera of a once mighty volcano and a second visit to the lighthouse. I had spotted the signs of the volcano on a satellite image of the Ardnamurchan peninsular on the internet when first planning the ride and had done some research confirming my suspicions about the origins of the three mile wide ring of hills. Nearly two years after that first discovery, this was the day when I would finally visit the place. I started by dropping right back to sea-level to do some shopping at Kilchoan Post Office. On the way I passed the remains of the unluckiest mouse in Scotland. On a road which sees a vehicle at most every fifteen minutes, it had managed to time its three second dash across the road to coincide with the passing of one of those vehicles and had been comprehensively flattened!

At the post office I bought spare batteries for the replacement camera, drinks to fill my bottle and some locally sourced midge repellent, the active ingredient of which was essence of bog myrtle! I figured that the natives must know a thing or two about keeping the little fiends at bay. *"The Lord in His wisdom invented the fly... And then forgot to tell us why".* We know now that he did so to save us from being swamped with dead creatures and debris but why did he invent the midge? To keep us humble? Suitably equipped, I headed back up the road towards the hotel and then branched off onto the even smaller road to Achnaha. This little hamlet of eight or ten homes is situated within the ring of hills which were the "roots" of the volcano when it was active sixty million years ago. The volcano is believed to have been a mile or more higher than the present landscape, so one and a half times the height of Ben Nevis these days and twice the height of Snowdon. The hills in the "ring" average a little over 1000 ft above sea level and are composed of gabbro, which is more resistant to corrosion than the surrounding rock and so have survived 60 million years of weather erosion slightly better.

*Looking back along my road into the caldera. The far distant hills are part of the outer ring and the middle distance ones are part of the main ring.*

*The continuation of the road crossing the caldera. South wall in the distance.*

Considering its unimaginably violent beginnings, it is a tranquil and beautiful place. Following instructions gleaned from the internet I stopped at a parking place a kilometre before Achnaha village and left the road to follow a path. I abandoned the bike fifty yards from the road, dumped the helmet with it and just took the camera with me on up the path until eventually I found my way onto the tallest of a line of small hills within the caldera. From this viewpoint, sitting on a convenient flat rock, I could see the road I had followed in from Achonich, a panoramic view of the caldera walls, an old, abandoned farmstead and the distant village of Achnaha.

A pair of eagles appeared on the hills of the north side and soared gracefully along the slopes round to the west – what wouldn't I have given to be able to join them in a glider. Someone else had the same idea, though in more dramatic style. I spotted his nose-light before I heard him – a Tornado high speed jet roared straight across the middle of the ring at a great rate of knots, not more than a few hundred feet above the higher crests. Fortunately he was alone and going in a straight line so within twenty seconds all was peace and quiet again.

I sat for a long time, trying to visualise the volcano towering a mile above where I was sitting and just absorbing the atmosphere of my surroundings. It took a long time to drag myself away. It's one of those places that grab you, above all rhyme or reason. Physically it's just a range of Scottish hills that happen to form a rough circle but to sit on this rock inside the circle was beyond my ability to conjure in words, so I shan't try. I suggest you go there sometime.

Eventually I did drag myself away, found the path back to the bike and wended my way down to the hotel for a late lunch. I was only two miles from the hotel when I was sitting in the caldera but it was nearly five miles by road to escape the encircling hills, drop nearly down to Kilchoan and then climb back up the road to the hotel on the outside of the main, complete ring of hills.

I sat in the bar and enjoyed a pleasant lunch and a pint with some of the regulars, rested for an hour to let it settle and then got my bits and pieces together to go and pay a second visit to the lighthouse.

*The three bands of hills. The, dark ones are part of the only complete ring.*

*An orange peel fungus – one of several growing in the caldera.*

*A poached copy of an aerial photograph of the caldera. ("N" = North).*
*My vantage point was the little dark hill at the top of the small central circle.*

*Two of the three engines in the plant room.*

On the road up to the lighthouse I spotted a car with a Herefordshire registration which I had seen during my travels in the morning. When it reached me I waved it down and asked the driver where he came from. He was a fellow cyclist from Ross-on-Wye, eleven miles from Ledbury. Another car came along the single-track road and so we had to part, but what a small world...

Reaching the Point of Ardnamurchan I found the visitor centre open and spent a pleasant hour exploring their exhibition, including the plant room where the compressed air for the giant fog horn was generated. There were three old diesel engines and the smell and paraphernalia took me straight back to my days as a power engineer with British Telecom. At one point I saw members of the public at the top of the lighthouse tower but by the time I'd finished in the visitor centre, the lighthouse door was firmly locked. There was no sign of a member of staff to ask about access.

Eventually, on a third visit to the tower, the door was open revealing a sign on the *inside* of the door stating that admission was by ticket available from the coffee shop. What coffee shop? I hadn't seen one. I found out that it was back down the road, outside the wall of the complex and I'd cycled past it on the way in. I leapt on the bike and rocketed down through the site to find the coffee shop. "Am I too late?" "Yes, I think you are" replied the lady, "Hang on – I'll check". She picked up her radio and asked Davie, who was at the top of the tower. "He says okay, if you're quick".

I was quick. I pedalled back up through the site, dumped the bike (carefully), grabbed camera and specs and probably broke the record for a 64 year-old climbing the 152 steps of Ardnamurchan lighthouse. Davie was already explaining things to two couples so I had the open air gallery to myself to recover my breath and pop off some photographs, including one of my trusty steed vertically below me. Back in the control room, Davie had finished his talk and was chatting to the two couples so I joined them. He gave me a potted version of the talk and slipped in various anecdotes as we went. Soon it was time to descend to ground level, much to the relief of the lady at the coffee shop who had a plumbing problem in the gents' toilet which she needed Davie to repair. I mounted the bike and got down there ahead of him to grab a cup of tea and a large slice of Victoria sponge.

I consumed my treats outside in the sunshine, chatting to a lady who was visiting with her daughter, son-in-law and her granddaughter, who was a little treasure and almost ready to take her first steps. I was last customer of the day at the coffee shop and so gave the waitress a hand taking in chairs and so on. I then spent half an hour sitting on the rocks, enjoying the view out to sea. After a few more photos it was time to pedal back to the Sonachan Hotel for dinner and to pack for the following morning's resumption of my travels. Twenty-four days after my visit, the lighthouse was to celebrate the 160th anniversary of its first operation.

Trip: 15.6                    Total: 256

*The lighthouse from the rocks.*

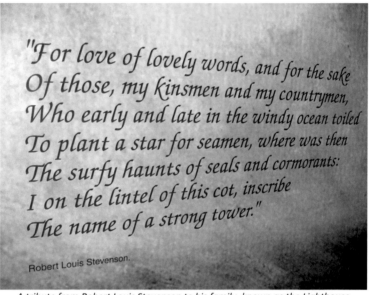

"For love of lovely words, and for the sake
Of those, my kinsmen and my countrymen,
Who early and late in the windy ocean toiled
To plant a star for seamen, where was then
The surfy haunts of seals and cormorants:
I on the lintel of this cot, inscribe
The name of a strong tower."

Robert Louis Stevenson.

*A tribute from Robert Louis Stevenson to his family, known as the Lighthouse Stevensons, and their workers. The engineer for the Ardnamurchan tower was Alan Stevenson.*

*An intense sunset from my bedroom window at Sonachan.*

Saturday 12<sup>th</sup> September.

## On With the Show

With a fair way to go I was on the road by 8.40 and cruising down to Kilchoan, where I had alighted from the ferry two days earlier. It was a beautiful morning; quite cool at that early hour, with mist and wispy cloud giving an ethereal quality to the landscape. Although I had completed the east to west journey – albeit a year late – and justified the sponsorship money which trusting folk had already paid me, I still had a week's travel to complete before returning home. My course this morning meandered a good deal but was due east overall for the first twenty miles or so to Salen and then, for the afternoon, more or less north although this being western Scotland, the road weaved around all over the place.

Beyond Kilchoan and the Tobermory ferry I was crossing new ground and on a classic Scottish morning, with clouds dancing around mountains and postcard-beautiful scenery, I was forever stopping to grab quick photographs. Consequently in the first hour I only covered 6.8 miles. (I have so many photographs of the scenery through which I passed that it has been difficult to choose which ones suit the small format of this book). Although the road skirted round the mountains and larger hills – hence the weaving around – it was far from flat but every slog up was rewarded with a chilly glide down the other side. All at once I started seeing the first signs of the approaching Autumn. Beech trees were turning gold at their extremities, bracken was already a rich brown and – outside the gatehouse of Glenborrodale Castle – I saw the first autumn crocuses. At one photo-stop I heard the call of a curlew and spotted a buzzard low and close by, prospecting for the first thermal of the day. I also saw what was becoming a regular sight on this trip: a hairy caterpillar bravely (or, if it failed in the attempt, foolhardily) crossing the road.

Not that the weather can be extreme up there but the roadside mail boxes have lift-up, storm-proof flaps on their slots rather like a domestic letter box. Acknowledgement by the Royal Mail of the inescapable fact of life in western Scotland that sometimes the rain flies horizontally, rather than falling! Happily, on this day it was doing neither.

*The morning view from my bedroom window. The flowers are montbretia.*

*Light clouds dancing around the mountains.*

*I had the road – and all of this – to myself.*

*The end of Loch Mudle, in the exact centre of the Ardnamurchan peninsular.*

*The view south-eastwards along Loch Sunart, near Laga.*

*Looking west along Loch Sunart towards the Atlantic Ocean.*

At Salen I turned north onto the A861, finally saying farewell to Loch Sunart after spending my morning following its northern shore. Having covered 22 bumpy miles I was half way through my planned 44 and would have stopped for coffee at the Salen Hotel but the sound of two (or more) noisy, precocious children dissuaded me. Inevitably, leaving the loch which is connected to the sea and therefore at sea-level, meant I had to begin to gain height. This road wandered around just like the one I'd followed along the loch but with more traffic, since it was an 'A' road. Finding a strong signal I seized the opportunity to swap texts with Sue and Ronny on the Isle of Skiathos.

Passing the end of Loch Shiel, I stopped at Acharacle for lunch at the Blue Parrot Tea Room (shades of Monty Python there) which was part of the village post office. They had been threatened with closure of the post office and so the community had taken it over and diversified to keep it viable. The tea room was part of that process and I was served a wholesome baguette and salad by Claire. Naughtily – but I could get away with it – I followed up with a large piece of scrumptious, moist, home-made, chocolate gateau. Just up the road, I waved to a gent who was sitting outside his cottage enjoying the sunshine. In response he raised his bottle of beer to me across the garden as if toasting me on my way.

A mile up the road I made a sharp right turn to head almost due east for several miles before turning back north-westwards over the intervening hump to drop down to Loch Moidart. Near the highpoint, I paused to investigate three cairns on a hillside just above the road, marked on the O/S map as "Captain Robertson's Cairn 1868". Subsequent research reveals much confusion about the history of the cairns but that the good captain is "believed to be Captain W J Robertson of the 42nd and 30th Regiment who died 26 June 1869". There is a suggestion that the actual, original Captain Robertson's Cairn was a fourth one which has since been demolished. In any event they are imposing structures and involved someone in some serious and skilful hard work at the time of their construction.

Along the side of Loch Moidart I passed the remains of a jetty which presumably once saw visits from paddle steamers since this is another sea-loch giving access to the Inner Hebrides. I couldn't think of any other reason for such a substantial structure.

*The three cairns, one of which may be Captain Robertson's.*

*The ruins of the old jetty on Loch Moidart.*

I started a long, steady ascent over the northern half of the Moidart peninsular. The road was mostly brand new and well engineered, having been part-funded by the EU. I was gradually seeing more of these long stretches of new road as I progressed into the Highlands and would see even more on the Isle of Skye. It was nice to see firm evidence of some EU money flowing back across the Channel in our direction. Eventually it was payback time and I had two long, glorious, arm-chilling swoops on the way down to sea-level once again at the Sound of Arisaig.

On my right through all of this was the vast wilderness of Lochaber, where the outdoor enthusiasts put large packs on their backs and walk for several days at a time, fording streams and camping out overnight or sleeping in remote bothies. Fortunately for my self esteem the area has no roads whatsoever, sparing me the need to justify taking the coward's way round the edge.

Having reached the sea again I turned east and, more or less, followed the shoreline to skirt Loch Ailort on en route to the settlement which shares its name – Lochailort. Unusually, I saw a herd of goats, including several kids, grazing freely on the side of the road. The last half dozen miles into Lochailort were a disappointment. The A861 was littered with caravan parks, as well as caravans and mobile homes just parked off the side of the carriageway wherever they could and tents pitched in amongst the trees and bushes. There was the general air of a "New Age" travellers' camp with the inevitable attendant litter. I suppose one can hardly blame the folk of Glasgow or wherever for heading west on a beautiful weekend.

A mile before my destination I was passed in the opposite direction by three replica 1950s grand prix cars. Two-seaters, they were far from cheap and the gentlemen driving them looked extremely pleased with themselves. I just looked envious though whether I could have fitted my 6' 4" frame into one of them must be doubtful. Now that the "official" part of my ride was complete I was allowed to cheat and on the following (Sunday) morning I planned to ride by train from Lochailort to Mallaig to catch the morning ferry over to the Isle of Skye. A visit to the station – no trains on Sundays – soon dashed that hope so I made my way to the Lochailort Inn, planning an early start.

The Lochailort Inn was brilliant and landlady Ellen welcomed me and settled me in. After the usual routine of shower, change, cup of tea I went down to the bar and enjoyed an excellent pint of Cairngorm Brewery's Trade Winds bitter, which was a treat after a dearth of real ales in recent days.

A gang of fly fishermen came in and set up camp at one end of the bar. They had obviously paid well for the privilege of casting their flies on whichever river they had fished and, once the malts were set up, their host / ghillie / guide was busy accepting fees and giving change. Well skilled in the arts of customer relations and hospitality and bearing a strong resemblance to the late Sir Compton McKenzie with his trim beard and deerstalker, he knew precisely who owed what and who was who.

My evening meal was delicious and landlord John didn't bat an eyelid when I explained my need for an early start the following morning – a Sunday. He just took it in his stride and said he'd be up anyway, which I'm not sure was the case. He runs a good ship.


Trip: 44.8          Total: 301


*"The wish to travel seems to me characteristically human: the desire to move, to satisfy your curiosity or ease your fears, to change the circumstances of your life, to be a stranger, to make a friend, to experience an exotic landscape, to risk the unknown..."*

*Paul Theroux*

Sunday 13<sup>th</sup> September.

# Over The Sea to Skye

John the landlord was true to his word and by 7.40 I was on the road with a full belly (he cooked an excellent breakfast) and a full drink bottle. The early start was necessary because the timetable showed the Skye ferry as due out of Mallaig – 18 miles away – at 9.45 and I needed to catch the early ferry because, after the crossing, I still had to cycle right across the bottom of the island to Kyleakin.

The first few miles set the pattern for the journey to Mallaig: half a mile of downhill, followed by a solid mile of gentle climb, then a long swoop downhill again. With the time factor I tried not to stop for photos but one or two just had to be taken. A big plus factor was the lack of wind, due to the early hour. Slogging up one particularly steep hill at 3.6 mph in second gear (out of 21) a sign instructed me to "Reduce Speed Now". I think not!

Having followed the south side of the Sound of Arisaig the previous afternoon, I was now paralleling the north side (cutting across various protuberances) before turning north for the eight mile run-in to Mallaig. I breached my normal modus operandi by ignoring a picturesque, meandering side road in favour of the "Main Drag" (i.e. the "A" road) in the interests of rapid progress. However, I still managed to grab a few photos of the misty islands to the west of me.

I completed 10.2 miles in the first hour, which I didn't think was too bad considering the early start and the hilly route. The north-westerly wind finally woke up a little after 9.00 and slowed my progress for the last two miles into Mallaig, where I arrived at 9.15. Enquiries revealed that the ferry actually left at 10.30 so all of the rush was for nothing and I could have departed an hour later or simply taken the scenic route on the journey. Never mind – now I had time to explore Mallaig, which I'd last visited in April 1978 with my Mum on her first and only visit to Scotland (36 hours out and back by train from Reading!). I was pleased to find a Co-op store open and took the chance stock up as usual on iron rations since legend had it that the Isle of Skye was closed on Sundays.

*Loch Nan Uamh (I'm not making these up – honestly!) at 7.58 am.*

*The cloud-capped Isle of Eigg (left) with the Isle of Rhum in the distance.*
*They are both visible from Ardnamurchan lighthouse.*

*Eigg (again) under its cap of cloud with Rhum peeping over the headland.*

The ferry crossing was uneventful apart from a strident alarm on one of the cars, which was sensitive to the movement of the boat and emitted a piercing whistle for 25 seconds, paused for 4 seconds and then started up again. It kept this up for more than half the journey until the crew relented ("Well, rules is rules...") and let the embarrassed owner of the car onto the forbidden turf of the car deck to strangle the thing. Apart from that the CalMac crew carried us economically, efficiently and safely across the water as ever. A nice touch on the larger vessels is an antiseptic foam dispenser in the public areas which is free for anyone to use. The foam disappears into the hands in seconds and obviously helps to prevent the spread of everyday bugs and diseases.

After disembarking at Armadale I enjoyed a cappuccino in a café outside the ferry terminal while the rest of the passengers dispersed and disappeared. The view back across to the mainland was breathtaking, with wisps of cloud clinging around the peaks of the higher mountains and the Sound of Sleat looking very calm and very cold in the early autumn sunshine. Enough daydreaming – peace and quiet had returned so it was time to apply myself to the road ahead.

With breakfast nearly five hours behind me, I was ready for an early lunch and so, only four and a half miles from the ferry terminal, I parked myself in a field gateway and set about eight slices of Leerdammer cheese, an apple and a drink from the bike bottle. I could imagine my Dad sitting beside me. When out cycling, he used to love to find a sheltered spot, out of the wind and with a good view, to have lunch. As a vegetarian he would have approved of my cheese in lieu of the usual pork pie, too. I don't believe he ever reached as far north as Skye but I know he would have enjoyed the view today.

Looking at the surrounding scenery, I could see why the Victorians became obsessed with the Scottish Highlands. The building of the railways in the mid-19th century quite suddenly gave them (the well-to-do ones, at any rate) relatively easy access to countryside which they couldn't have dreamed of previously. To them the unique mountain light and scenery must have seemed like Heaven on Earth. Artists like Charles W. Oswald and Francis Jamieson became obsessed with creating Scottish landscape paintings, many of which are still familiar to us today.

*A couple enjoy the sunshine and the tranquillity of the Sound of Sleat.*

*My lunch stop at the entrance to a small, loch-side field.*

In the pleasant sunshine I settled into reflective mood. I wondered whether the early inhabitants – the Picts, Scots and Celts – appreciated all this scenic beauty as we do. Or were they too busy scratching a living to give it a thought? Bearing in mind that they would have nothing to compare it with, was it just where they lived? Was a fine, sunny day like this just a pelt drying day or a day to turn the hay? Certainly they populated the clouds and mountain tops with mystical beings and they must have wondered about whoever lived in those glens and mountains across the water.

Back in the present, the sky (over Skye!) was more or less cloudless, though over on the mainland there was uniform, flat cloud cover only six or eight miles inland from the coast. As I was clearing up wrappers and so on I noted that I had just consumed 716 calories of Leerdammer. That should keep me going for a while, then… A little later, as I turned inland, Skye's own sheet of high cloud began to obscure the sun. Not a bad thing as the road ascended away from the coast and for a while I had some work to do. After a few undulations I had the usual long, fast freewheel down to the main road on the north side of the island. I ventured a little way off-route towards Broadford but it wasn't very exciting so as soon as the road began to drop, which would mean uphill on the return, I turned back and headed towards Kyleakin.

An hour's gentle pedalling saw me coasting into the village. As expected, I found the White Heather Hotel at the very far end of Kyleakin, by the harbour. I was greeted by landlady Gillian who despite her protestations to the contrary, had the organisation of the hotel down to a fine art. An ex-schoolteacher, the amount of information about house rules and what to see and do locally that she could cram into a welcome chat was phenomenal. She and husband Craig had everything well set up and nothing was too much trouble.

Once I'd settled in I wandered through Kyleakin and onto the beach to watch the sun set behind the Skye Bridge. I had booked dinner at the village's main pub since the one thing Gillian and Craig didn't provide was an evening meal. Came time to eat and I found that, even on the Isle of Skye, the waiters and waitresses were all east-European. The meal was very nice – although the place lacked any sort of ambience – with a glass of Californian rosé in the absence of real ale.

*The outskirts of Kyleakin, with the mainland beyond the boats to the left.*

*The Skye Bridge which sadly, I think, superseded the old, more romantic ferry.*

*Last light over Skye with a finger of low cloud creeping between the hills.*

After forty five years of mispronunciation I discovered that the village is Kyle-a(r)kin and not Ky-leak-in, as I had always thought. It is named after the Viking King Haakon, who sailed through the sound on the way to being defeated in battle further down the coast. There is a tradition that in his days an old lady had a chain stretched right across the sound and no boat could pass until it had paid a toll. She would then lower the chain into the water to allow the boat to pass.

I can see several flaws in that story. Where, in those days, did she obtain a chain of that length – getting on for half a mile – and where did she obtain the strength to raise and lower it?
Once again... I think not! It's a good story though.


Trip:  40          Total:  341


"A journey, after all, neither begins in the instant we set out, nor ends when we have reached our door step once again. It starts much earlier and is really never over, because the film of memory continues running on inside of us long after we have come to a physical standstill. Indeed, there exists something like a contagion of travel, and the disease is essentially incurable."

Ryszard Kapuściński.

Monday 14<sup>th</sup> September.

## A Little Self Indulgence

Today was my third day off from journeying – one more than the original timetable due to being stranded on the Isle of Arran. I planned to explore Kyleakin and revisit one or two places on the mainland which I remembered from the 1960s. The sky was cloudless, apart from the edge of something peeping over the southern horizon. I rode over the bridge, missing the romance of the old ferry, and went into Kyle of Lochalsh to top up my wallet and my drink bottle. Having done both I set off up the road to Plockton, the location for the 1990s TV series "Hamish Macbeth".

My previous visit to the area had been 45 years earlier and I had forgotten how hilly the road was. It's more or less constantly rising and falling, and steeply at that, so on a warm, still morning I was soon rather warm myself. Layers of clothing were shed. Plockton being located on an inlet from the sea, the final approach was downhill and quite suddenly I found myself joining lots of other sightseers in the village at the water's edge. Because of the TV series it's now on the tourist coach trail and there were people queuing for Callum's Seal Boat Trips, people fussing over camera settings, people looking for toilets, etc. There weren't enough people to stop me capturing some nice shots of the village. An open canoe hove into view on the water and made its way round to the slipway where a young couple disembarked. As a fellow open canoeist I felt quite envious and wandered over to chat to them. We spent half an hour comparing notes and experiences of canoeing and Scotland.

As I was on a day off I decided to indulge myself and ride back to Kyle on the train, having failed to ride the rails the previous morning. I went to the excellent village chippy and waited while they cooked me a haddock supper (at lunchtime!) which I toted, wedged in my handlebar bag, up the hill to the railway station. I sat on the platform in glorious sunshine and ate it while waiting for the train, along with half a dozen boisterous teenagers. Both chips and fish were delicious and not overly fatty. It was standing room only on the train, which must be good news for a line which has been threatened with closure more than once.

*Two views from the waterfront in Plockton*

*The tip of Kyleakin, with the Skye Bridges beyond, viewed from Castle Moil.*

Back in Kyle of Lochalsh I visited the Friends of The Kyle Line shop on the station, looked at their small exhibition, bought a few trinkets and then crossed to the gift shop at the Tourist Information Centre where I bought Sue a pair of earrings. Being on a bike, with limited storage space, the range of gifts one can purchase is sadly limited.

I took a slow ride back to the hotel, picked up my journal and sat on the harbour wall writing up the day's happenings. That occupied me for a while before I became restless, swapped the journal for the camera and went to explore Castle Moil, on the other side of the harbour mouth. This entailed walking back down the harbour inlet towards the village, crossing a bridge and returning along the south side, opposite the hotel. As it was near high tide there was some scrambling over rocks but nothing too serious. By the time I'd mounted the small hill on which the castle stands, I was glowing and breathing well. There is too little of the castle left to be that interesting but the views are splendid. I gleaned the following information from the Ealahol website after returning home:

*"In the late 15th century Clan Mackinnon moved from their earlier base at Dun Ringill, near Elgol, to this castle at Kyleakin. At that time the castle was known as Dun Acainn. Early in the 17th century the clan moved on and the castle fell into disrepair. All that remains is this ruin, looking from some angles rather like a massive decaying tooth!"*

Returning from the castle I met a pair of local fishermen and asked them about the Vanguard, a large tugboat which was anchored in a decrepit condition at the back of the harbour. They told me that it had sunk whilst towing a submarine to Canada but Gillian later qualified that. She said that it had been involved in NATO exercises and had sunk due to the ineptitude of the skipper ("He managed to sink it!"). Under normal circumstances it would have been left where it was but the Navy insisted on doing things by the book and it was salvaged. Kyleakin was the nearest place where it could be left. Apparently Highland Council had put up £30,000 towards the cost of bringing it back into use but a) it was stuffed with asbestos, b) having lain on its side on the seabed for a while the engine room in particular was in a terrible state and c) still partly full of sea water, it was rotting from the inside outwards. The clincher was that the insurers didn't want to know.

*Castle Moil or Casteal Maol, as it's called in Gaelic.*

*The tug Vanguard with Castle Moil behind.*

The conclusion to the story comes inevitably from the Internet – Fount of All Knowledge. The following synopsis was poached from the report of the Marine Accident Investigation Board:

*"A 39-metre sea going tug was taking a familiar passage on the north-coast of a Scottish island in order to rendezvous with a vessel. During the passage the skipper decided to take an inshore route between the island and some rocks and shoal patches that were a few cables offshore. This was unnecessary, as there was plenty of time to follow the normal route that took the vessel well clear of all dangers. The skipper did not know his precise position and the vessel grounded on a submerged rock, which was to port of the track he had intended to take. He put the engine astern and was able to get clear. The passage was resumed, but a new course was chosen to pass well clear of dangers.*

*The engine room flooded and about half an hour later the vessel was deliberately grounded on a gently rocky shore on the island of Rona. The crew were evacuated safely to boats, but after a while the vessel listed over and was a constructive total loss".*

Silly Billy! The report simply advised that the skipper undertook a navigation course and tried to do better next time. Whether his employers had sterner words for him, or if he even kept his job, who knows? The accident happened on September 7th 2004 and the Vanguard sat in Kyleakin harbour until its removal for scrapping six months after I saw it. It looked a sorry sight and, whilst regretting that it couldn't be saved and restored, I'm glad it's no longer lying there rotting away. It's amazing how long bureaucracy can take to reach a practical conclusion.

Having had a substantial breakfast followed by that haddock supper and having had an easy day, I didn't need dinner so when the light began to fade I retired to my room and snacked as I completed the journal entry.

Trip: 12.6          Total: 354

*"Once the travel bug bites there is no known antidote, and I know that I shall be happily infected until the end of my life"*

*Michael Palin*

Tuesday 15<sup>th</sup> September.

# The Road From the Isles

I awoke to a marked change in the weather, with a uniform covering of grey cloud and no hint of sunshine. The benevolent anticyclone which had been keeping the weather settled for me had divided in two, allowing a weakening occluded front (the weather man said) to creep through the gap. After another good breakfast from Craig and Gillian I rode out through Kyleakin, under a huge, black cloud which made it dark enough to bring on the automatic streetlights. However, by the time I'd crossed the bridge and topped up with essentials in Kyle of Lochalsh it was 11.40 and the cloud was showing signs of moving on.

My route out of town followed the "A" road along the mainland side of Loch Alsh. As ever in western Scotland the road doesn't stay at sea level but seizes every opportunity to ascend to a great height (in cycling terms, anyway). This is the fabled Road To The Isles (or rather *From* the Isles in my case!) and, similarly to the Ring of Kerry in southern Ireland, carries a steady procession of coaches filled with people sitting inside gazing out.

A little under an hour brought me to Dornie and a place I'd wanted to revisit for 45 years – Eilean Donan Castle. As a 19 year-old on my first solo cycle tour in 1964, I had rounded a bend in the road and found this imposing castle, in its beautiful setting jutting out into Loch Duich, standing in the morning sunshine before me. Although it is the star of a million calendars and a further million biscuit tins and chocolate boxes, I had never seen it and was mightily impressed.

I was amazed now to find that the castle had been rebuilt from a total ruin in the 20<sup>th</sup> Century after 200 years as little more than a pile of rubble. I took the tour. It takes an hour or so to explore the inside of the castle and I found it very interesting. One is left to one's own devices, with friendly staff on hand to answer questions if required. It is run very much like a National Trust house but is independent and therefore a little cheaper. Much history was put across very effectively and the reconstruction of a 1932 kitchen, with life-sized figures and realistic food "cooking" made my mouth water.

Back outside the sky was still broken cloud with patches of sunshine so I retrieved my bike and scooted down to the overflow car park, which was completely deserted and had a good view of the castle. I sat on a grassy bank, got out the lunch which I'd bought in Kyle and settled down to wait for the right splash of sunshine to strike the castle.

I finished my lunch and revelled in the luxury of being able to sit, watch the tide come in and enjoy the scene. A gaggle of a hundred or more gulls had gathered on the surface of the loch behind me and I watched every other gull within sight home in on them. Thanks to Sir David Attenborough and his intrepid film crews, I could clearly visualise the seething shoal of fish below the surface, on which they were feeding.

Spotting a large patch of blue sky drifting over the hill towards the sun, I started to suss good camera angles. Then the castle was bathed in sunlight and seemed to come to life. I took several photos, safe in the ability to sift them on the computer when I got home. A middle aged couple had joined me in the car park and were also taking photos. I said to the gentleman "I've waited an hour and a half for this sunshine". They both looked blank and apologetic and then he said something in French. I scratched through forty eight years of rust on my schoolboy French and told them again in their own language. Their faces lit up and he shook my hand but, fortunately for me, didn't try to start a conversation. We stumbled through a few pleasantries and then parted. But parted as friends – *vive l'Entente Cordiale*.

After a long break, it was time to catch up on some miles. I mounted the bike and moved stiffly out onto the road and turned east. The road was very winding, with no overtaking opportunities, and it was noticeable that traffic came along in mini-convoys of half a dozen or so vehicles as each slow-moving one gathered up the faster ones coming up behind. An MPV passed me and on the spare wheel cover was the slogan "Campers – Nature's way of feeding mosquitoes".

I took on some serious climbing now, as I left Loch Duich behind and headed up Glen Shiel into the mountains. Approaching the site of the 1719 Battle of Glen Shiel I spotted a section of the old, single track road down which I cycled, aged 19, in 1964. It was quite nostalgic thinking back to that first ever solo, independent holiday. I wonder what I'd have thought then if someone had told me that I'd be cycling through there again at the age of 64.

Sadly, near the top of the glen I passed two dead deer within a hundred yards of each other. Eventually the endless uphill slog ceased to be endless and I was at the top. Some measure of reward followed as I freewheeled for a mile and a half to my overnight stop, the Cluanie Inn, which is located in the middle of nowhere. Reception was deserted and after hanging around for five minutes with no sign of life, I hunted around the hotel until I found the landlady, who returned with me to reception to book me in and show me to my room, which was very pleasant. The window looked out onto a causeway crossing the head of Loch Cluanie with the loch beyond.

*The modern road heading up into Glen Shiel...*

*...and, on the right here, the old road (now a footpath) going down.*

Having showered and changed I drank my cup of tea while taking a longer look from the window. A gentleman with a large Springer spaniel was walking purposefully along the causeway away from the road and towards the mountains. The dog, running free, dashed to and fro across the heather and was in seventh heaven, looking as if it was being propelled by its tail, which waved in huge, ecstatic circles. Half an hour later they returned, with the dog now on a lead. The spaniel still had enough energy to make the man put in some effort to avoid being pulled flat onto his face. They were both clearly loving it. I discovered later that the causeway is the beginning of a long-distance wilderness path and at the entrance it has a warning sign discouraging ill-equipped visitors from getting out of their depth and into trouble. I also discovered that the gentleman was the father of the landlady.

Downloading data from my handlebar computer, I found that the 30.3 miles I had covered had taken me only two hours and fifty six minutes of cycling, meaning that I had averaged over 10 mph despite the long slog into the mountains from sea level.

Trip:  30.3          Total: 384

*Home from home in the wilderness: the Cluanie Inn.*

Wednesday 16th September.

## Dumplings and Heroes.

I woke to a beautiful, misty morning with shafts of sunlight filtering down through the clouds and playing around the mountains surrounding Loch Cluanie. The scene was constantly changing as the movement of the clouds was reflected in the consequent movement of the sunbeams across the landscape. After leaving the Cluanie Inn I was cycling along the side of the loch when I was overtaken by a powerful, 2-seater aircraft doing around 200 knots at half the height of the surrounding mountains and only a few hundred feet above the water. He was having to bank steeply to follow the curves of the loch and was probably pretending he was in a Spitfire. I envied him more than you can imagine. I'd seen him the previous day over Skye and Kyle of Lochalsh and assumed he was on a business trip but this was clearly for fun.

There was some residual cloud from the previous day but it was gradually dissolving as the high pressure re-asserted itself. In my mirror I saw a large timber truck with trailer coming up behind me on a long, blind (for him) bend. As I could see round the corner I gave him my usual wave to come on through because the road beyond the bend was clear of on-coming traffic. As he passed he tooted a thank-you on his air horns, roared on up the road and left me with a lovely smell of pine resin.

Reaching the end of Loch Cluanie I discovered why its water level was so low after an exceptionally wet summer. I had forgotten that it is a dammed loch, feeding a hydro-electric generator, and they can control water levels according to the demand for electricity. A mile after passing the dam, I forsook the Inverness road and followed the A87 hard right towards Fort William. The road began to climb and did so for four miles solid, rising above the end of Loch Loyne. As I passed the access road to the Loch Loyne dam a Landrover was driving down towards the dam (another hydro-electric one). A further mile up the road I stopped to take some photos of the Loch and there on the dam were two white-overalled figures, standing in the sunshine watching the water flow through the dam. I imagined them earlier, sitting in the office and saying "It's a beautiful day. We'd better pop up and make sure the Loch Loyne dam is still there…"

*Morning light.*

*Loch Cluanie.*

Turning south-east I immediately reaped the reward for my recent labours – more than four miles of freewheeling, most of it at over 30 mph. This swift blast brought me to the Glengarry Community Hall, where a sign invited me to visit their café. That seemed like an eminently sensible idea! Inside I found three ladies serving freshly made tea and coffee and a mouth-watering selection of home-made cakes. I settled for coffee and a slice of spicy fruit dumpling. The dumpling was so nice that I asked how it was made. The lady who had made it started to tell me but then invited me into their kitchen while she found pen and paper to write down the full recipe. I include it here for anyone who would care to give it a go. The result should be delicious.

A couple of miles down the road, the A87 joined the A82, originally one of General Wade's Military Roads, and I turned south-west down the Great Glen towards Spean Bridge, where I was to spend the night. Approaching Laggan I had an opportunity to escape the main road with its attendant traffic and take a trail which followed the west side of Loch Lochy. I had reserved my decision until I saw it at first hand. Once at the beginning of the trail, it didn't take long. Firstly there was a sign like the one by the Cluanie Inn, warning me that I was entering a wilderness area etc and secondly a mountain biker emerged from the trail caked in mud and breathing hard. The main road for me then...

The A82 crosses the Caledonian Canal via a manned swing bridge and as I crossed the bridge the operator, a guy of around 50, was sitting in his control cabin playing a guitar in the absence of any boats requiring his attention. I didn't see any boats travelling on the canal all of the time I was alongside it so he must have had a lot of practise. As lunchtime approached a sign lured me down to have a drink at "The Only Floating Pub on the Caledonian Canal". Just what I needed. I followed the signs and, needless to say, when I reached it the pub was closed.

I saw the Rich Man in a Fast Plane three more times during the morning and I came round to the idea that he may have been a working pilot earning a living flying other (rich) men around the Highlands for *their* enjoyment. I was still green with envy. Following the shores of Loch Lochy, which lies along the Great Glen geological fault line, the scenery was much less dramatic than it had been for the past week. This was ironic when I was rapidly approaching the highest mountain in Britain, Ben Nevis.

# Spicy Fruit Dumpling

## Ingredients:

6 ozs  Self-raising flour
3 ozs  Atora
6 ozs  Breadcrumbs
1 tsp  Grated ginger
2 tsp  Cinnamon
1 tsp  Baking soda
2 tbsp  Syrup
1½ cup  Milk
4ozs  Soft brown sugar
10ozs  Mixed fruit

## Equipment:

A large saucepan or a catering size boiling pan.
A cotton cloth large enough to wrap the mixture.
String to tie the cloth.

## Method:

Mix all of the ingredients in a large bowl.

Boil the cloth for a few minutes in the pan, remove and allow to cool until safe to handle.

Wrap the mixture in the cloth, squeeze tightly and tie the top with the string.

Place carefully in the boiling water, bring back to the boil and simmer for three hours.

**NB:** If using a saucepan, the water will need topping up with hot water from a kettle periodically – **Check regularly.**

After three hours lift the wrapped dumpling from the pan, stand it in a colander in the sink and allow to drain for a minute or two.

Untie and open the top of the cloth, place an inverted plate on top and carefully turn the whole thing over, then remove the cloth.

*Recipe cadged from the ladies in the kitchen at the Glengarry Community Centre, Invergarry, Inverness-shire.*

I spotted the nose light of a Tornado fast jet coming towards me over the water at low level – now this *was* rapid – and just had time to grab a photo. If he happened to cross paths with the two-seater it would put things in perspective since the jet was travelling at more than twice their speed.

Having been let down by the floating pub I found a gate near the side of the road which led onto a quiet hillside. The sun was shining from a clear blue sky so, in the absence of any midges, I seized the moment and stripped to the waist while I ate the picnic lunch which the Cluanie Inn had provided. It was fine until I got to the apple, which was a French Golden Delicious. As we all know the only accurate part of that description is the word French, since they are green and sharp. I took one bite to clean my teeth, grimaced and heaved the rest into the undergrowth for re-cycling. I had found – or been guided to – a delightful spot, screened from the road by trees and far enough away to spare me the noise of the traffic. The silence suddenly registered the fact that I was the only living being there. One has to assume that the ground and vegetation were seething with bugs and microbes, some of them traumatised by the unexpected arrival of a French Golden Delicious, but there was hardly a single animal or bird, not even in the vast sky. The exception that proved the rule was a solitary spider which was in the early stages of building its latest web. I could see what it was doing but, for the life of me, I couldn't see how it was doing it. No doubt Sir David Attenborough could have told me. No doubt he and his men have filmed the process at some time.

A long ascent brought me to the Commando Memorial above Spean Bridge, which greatly impressed me when I first saw it in 1964. Originally it commemorated commandos who died in World War Two, having trained in this area. These days a Garden of Remembrance has been created close by to remember commandos lost in more recent conflicts in the Middle East. In that circular garden were many tributes to fallen commandos and maybe fifteen visitors, many of whom would be remembering their comrades or relatives. The atmosphere was respectful rather than sombre and completely different from my visit in 1964, when I was the only person there. Today there were around forty people, including those at the Garden of Remembrance. As I was preparing to leave, a Tornado jet passed over quite low and very fast, rocked its wings in salute and was gone in seconds. Very moving.

Waiting to cross the traffic back onto the A82 I had a quick chat to two young ladies who were part of a larger group of cyclists and in the last stages of a Land's End – John O'Groats ride. Then, delightedly, I freewheeled for a mile and a half off the hill into Spean Bridge village. I found a shop beside the burnt out shell of the Scotch Whisky Centre (that must have burned well) and filled up the empty bike bottle, had a snack and bought a bottle of Cairngorm Brewery Trade Winds as an insurance against a dry evening.

I hunted around for the Aonach Mor Hotel, where I had a room booked, and couldn't find it. Eventually I asked a local and discovered that it was on the approaches to the village and I had therefore rocketed past it on my gleeful descent from the hill. When I found it, it was a fairly unprepossessing 1960s place. However, the welcome was warm and I was able to sit in the sunshine on the back lawn and write up the journal over my cup of tea. The room was very basic and the only other guest was a long-term resident who was on some kind of contract job and was away from the hotel from 5.30am until 7.30 in the evening. The food was simple fare but nicely prepared. The only ale was chemical fizz so I waited and savoured my pint of Trade Winds Ale from the tooth mug back in my room.

Trip:  37.4          Total:  392

*"To move, to breathe, to fly, to float,*
*To gain all while you give,*
*To roam the roads of lands remote,*
*To travel is to live."*

*Hans Christian Andersen*

# Friday 17th September.

## The last Leg.

I had a mere 8 miles to cover to Fort William, with a slight downhill gradient most of the way. I would like to have escaped the main road traffic by following the B8004 down the west side of the River Lochy but this would have entailed retracing my steps(?) back up the long hill to the Commando Memorial. That early in the day I simply couldn't rustle up the enthusiasm and so, with the huge bulk of Ben Nevis looming over me, I set off down the A82.

About half way to Fort William I changed down a cog to deal with an up-slope, felt the gear lever go slack in my hand and found myself struggling in top gear instead! I spotted a lay-by a short distance up the road and heaved along to it to investigate. It didn't take long to establish that my rear gear changer cable had broken at the handlebar end. Unlike a wheel end break this was not something which could be fixed at the roadside. By jiggling one of the adjusting screws I was able to set the rear changer to middle gear, giving me the choice of three gears via the front changer. There was a time when three gears was the most that any cyclist had available to them, so this would certainly suffice for me to trolley four easy miles into Fort William. It began to dawn on me how lucky I had been. Over the past fortnight I had passed through some remote areas where I would have been over eighty miles from any cycle shop, let alone one that stocked the relevant cable. Without my full twenty one gears I would have had to work a lot harder, modify my route to get to a bike shop and walk up a great many hills. I made a mental note to replace the front changer cable and – more importantly – both brake cables, which were all of the same age, when I got home.

On the outskirts of the town I passed a touching memorial to cyclist Jason MacIntyre, who had been killed in an accident there the previous year. As always, this made me aware of my own vulnerability and my reliance on the road-craft of every motorist I encountered along the way. These memorials are erected at the sites of fatal cycling accidents by an international volunteer organisation called Ghost Bikes (www.Ghostbikes.org).

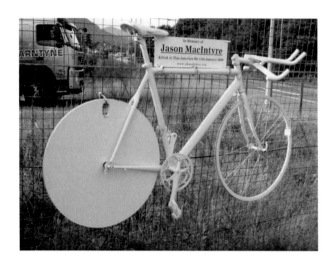

In Fort William I sought out the town's main cycle shop, Off Beat Bikes. I negotiated a deal whereby I would leave the bike, saddlebag and handlebar bag with them all day and they would replace the gear cable for me. This was the perfect arrangement for me as I had been wondering where I could leave the bike for the day while I gift shopped and got re-acquainted with Fort William. First task was to go up to the railway station and ensure that no nasty surprises awaited me with regard to the Fort William Sleeper. The train was already in the station, its four carriages being prepared for the journey to London so I grabbed a photograph, since it would be nearly dark when I came to back to board it.

After Edinburgh the Sleeper only called at Preston and Crewe on its way south to London so I was booked to Crewe, where I could catch a train to Hereford and thence to Ledbury.

*Oh Mr Porter, what shall we do?*
*I want to go to Birmingham*
*But you only stop at Crewe.*

Having established that all was as I hoped at the station I went to find myself a decent cup of coffee. I walked the whole length of the main street without finding anything very appealing and so ended up back by the railway station at Nevisport, an excellent outdoor shop. They have a good restaurant/café where I found my cup of coffee plus a slice of their irresistible walnut cake.

The rest of the morning was spent wandering around Fort William and buying small gifts to take home for Sue. In 1965, the last time I was in Fort William, the town resounded to the sound of bagpipes. In 2009 the music was provided by two colourful Andean gentlemen playing drum and panpipes. Between tunes I thrilled to the sight of one of them reaching under his traditional Peruvian costume, coming out with a mobile phone and sending a text. I found an excellent bakery selling all sorts of "home-baked" goodies. Choosing a couple of filled rolls, an apple pie and a cold drink I went to enjoy the sunshine in the park and watch the world go by. After lunch I spent an interesting couple of hours exploring the town museum.

Then I worked my way down to Off Beat Bikes to collect the bike and bags. They had replaced the broken gear cable, straightened the gear carrier which, at some time in the past, had become twisted and tuned the gears so that they ran more smoothly than they had for ages. All this cost me under £12 including the new cable – a lot less than I was expecting and great value for money.

The idle day had left me feeling lethargic so, having regained my steed I thrashed up and down the Fort William by-pass several times to wake myself up and get the feel of the newly overhauled gears. I clocked up about five miles, pausing only to take a couple of photographs down Loch Linnhe from the bottom end of the town, and felt much better for it.

Eventually, with the shops all closing, I made my way up to the railway station, secured the bike and went over to the adjacent hypermarket where I had a very reasonably priced meal in the restaurant. Back at the station I had an hour to sit and watch the daylight fade before the platform opened to allow passengers onto the train. On the station wall was a commendation plaque "Awarded to the Area Manager and staff of Fort William Station in recognition of their exceptional efforts during the severe blizzard conditions in January and February 1984 to clear the line and keep [rail] traffic moving". It was good to see official recognition of people's loyalty.

I had reserved a first class sleeper cabin as this was the only way to avoid the uncertainties of sharing a two-berth cabin with a total stranger. Whilst it was unlikely to be Jack the Ripper or Julian Clary, I was prepared to pay extra to avoid the possibility of a snorer, a compulsive talker or someone who needed to pee every three hours. I have to say that ScotRail know how to look after first class passengers. Waiting in cabin G7 was a tasteful mini duffel bag containing everything a weary traveller could want – eye mask, bed-socks, facecloth, cotton buds, cotton wool balls, cleansing pad, tooth brush & paste, razor & shaving cream, deodorant spray and moisturiser cream.

Before retiring for the night one could sit in armchair comfort in the first class lounge or summon the attendant to the cabin with the press of a button. I chose the lounge, where I enjoyed two pints of Adnams' Bitter and a cup of hot chocolate (how the rich do live!) as we crossed Rannoch Moor in the darkness and meandered down towards the Clyde, passing Gareloch nuclear submarine base along the way.

I was a little disappointed not to be able see Rannoch Moor, simply because it really is total wilderness and unique in Britain, as I found out when I cycled across it twice in 1964 and once more in '65. Looking out into the night from the train there was simply a great blackness, occasionally punctuated by the lights of a car on the good old A82, with which we were re-united at the southern edge of the moor.

Apparently the moor was created by the retreat of a glacier around twenty thousand years ago. It is so bleak, swampy and impenetrable that I should imagine there must be parts of it which have never felt the tread of a human foot. In ancient times it was forested and I recall seeing the preserved remains of tree stumps when I cycled across it. You can get some idea of the place by looking at the aerial views available on the internet on Google Maps etc. Billy Connolly's description of MAMBA (Miles And Miles of Bugger All) was never more applicable.

Trip:  13.3          Total:  405

*"We live in a wonderful world that is full of beauty, charm and adventure. There is no end to the adventures we can have if only we seek them with our eyes open."*

Jawaharlal Nehru

18<sup>th</sup> September.

# Home Run.

At Waverley St Station Edinburgh, while I slumbered, our train was split in two as we lost the diesel locomotive and the two non-sleeper carriages (in one of which was my bike). We were amalgamated into the Inverness Sleeper's fourteen carriages to make a train of sixteen carriages. Fortunately part of this process involved the cabin attendant removing my bike from the guard's compartment of its detached carriage while I slept and placing it in the guard's compartment of the new, very long Caledonian Sleeper.

The train took just over nine hours to reach Crewe from Fort William because the drivers of both the diesel and then the electric locomotives proceeded very gently in deference to their sleeping passengers. There were sixteen station stops along the way and, almost without exception, the stops and starts were conducted very smoothly and with great decorum. By the time my cabin attendant gave a wake-up tap on the compartment door I was already awake and dressed and gratefully accepted the makings of a pot of tea. I had declined breakfast as 4.30 was simply too early for my digestive system. I had prepared my own breakfast pack from bits and pieces bought from the Fort William hypermarket and this was to be consumed at a more civilised hour on the train from Crewe to Hereford.

Shortly before 5.00 am we pulled into Crewe and I emerged onto a dark, desolate platform with saddlebag, handlebar bag, helmet and drink bottle. The guard's compartment was no longer in the next carriage but one – it was ten carriages up the train! Happily there was a long stop since the locomotive was scheduled for a crew change and I had time to carry my gear up to the guard's compartment, find it locked, go twelve carriages back down the train to find the guard, return with him to the compartment, wait for him to unlock it and retrieve the bike.

From this point the journey took a downturn. I had to wait a chilly hour on the deserted Crewe Station for the train to Hereford and an hour and three quarters later that train – running on time – brought me into Hereford a few minutes after the Ledbury train had departed! This left me with a further hour and a quarter to kill before the next train was due.

I lingered over a cup of coffee and a newspaper at the station café. Eventually the train arrived and whisked me along the line to Ledbury. Between leaving the Caledonian Sleeper at Crewe and reaching Ledbury I spent equal amounts of time travelling and sitting around waiting for trains. Back under my own steam again, I quickly pedalled the mile and a half up the hill to home, shower and washing machine. Sue was still enjoying the sunshine on the Isle of Skiathos and wouldn't be home until the following day.

*Safely home again.*
*My trusty golly saddlebag mascot and rear lookout, veteran of Lowestoft to Land's End, Lowestoft to Carlisle and now - together with Sue's Moroccan good luck charms - of Carlisle to Fort William via Ardnamurchan Point and Skye.*